Educating the Nigerian Child

Educating the Nigerian Child

Amina Titi Atiku Abubakar

Spectrum Books Limited
Ibadan
Abuja •Benin City •Lagos •Owerri

Spectrum titles can be purchased on line at
<u>www.spectrumbooksonline.com</u>

Published by
Spectrum Books Limited
Spectrum House
Ring Road
PMB 5612
Ibadan, Nigeria
e-mail: admin1@spectrumbooksonline.com

in association with
Safari Books (Export) Limited
1st Floor
17 Bond Street
St Helier
Jersey JE2 3NP
Channel Islands
United Kingdom

Europe and USA Distributor
African Books Collective Ltd
The Jam Factory
27 Park End Street
Oxford OX1, 1HU, UK

© Amina Titi Atiku Abubakar

First published, 2003

All rights reserved. This book is copyright and so no part of it may be reproduced, stored in a retrieval system, or transmitted, in any form or by any means, electronic, mechanical, electrostatic, magnetic tape, photocopying, recording or otherwise, without the prior written permission of the copyright owner.

ISBN: 978-029-422-8

Printed by Printmarks Ventures, Ososami, Ibadan

CONTENTS

	Page
Foreword	vii
Preface	ix
Acknowledgement	xi

CHAPTER ONE
Education and Philosophy — 1

CHAPTER TWO
Nigeria and the Rights of the Child — 16

CHAPTER THREE
Child Education — 29

CHAPTER FOUR
Stages of Child Development — 57

CHAPTER FIVE
Improving Child Education — 79

CHAPTER SIX
Social Vices and Violence — 120

CHAPTER SEVEN
Philosophy and Policy Formulation — 145

CHAPTER EIGHT
Equipment and Materials for Schools   163

CHAPTER NINE
Financing and Budgeting   184

CHAPTER TEN
What Sort of Future?   198

Index   229

FOREWORD

This book is written essentially to satisfy the needs and aspirations of anyone who is interested in the growth and development of the child. The teacher, businessman, nurse, doctor, and in fact, any professional, would find portions of this book both relevant and interesting.

This book is unique in three respects. Firstly, the author is keenly interested in children and their upbringing, which would serve as a springboard for being good citizens and leaders. Secondly, the language of the text is simple and down-to-earth. Thirdly, the book is handy and affordable.

Much care has been taken to include contemporary issues that are of interest to most people. I sincerely recommend the book to all who are concerned about our children.

ALHAJI ATIKU ABUBAKAR
VICE PRESIDENT
FEDERAL REPUBLIC OF NIGERIA

PREFACE

This book is a reflection of the author's interest and concern for the development of the Nigerian child. For many decades, the author has been interested in ensuring that the Nigerian child is brought up in a way that would enhance his future leadership abilities. The book covers a wide variety of topics. No matter your background or specialisation, you will find various aspects of this book useful.

The book is composed of ten chapters. Chapter one deals with education and philosophy. It answers such questions as what is education? What is man? What is truth? It also examines the importance of education to the Nigerian child.

Chapter two is on Nigeria and the rights of the child. It considers some of the rights of the child adopted by the General Assembly of the United Nations on November 20, 1989. Other topics contained in this chapter are; child study, innate tendencies of man, behaviour of the child and what to do as a teacher and when.

Chapter three deals with child education. It considers early childhood education, nature and extent of programmes as well as learning and development. It considers Erikson's stages of psycho-social development and Piaget's stages of cognitive development. It also offers their educational implications.

The stages of child development are considered in chapter four. It deals with physical development as well as the influence of heredity and environment on physical development. It also considers intelligence and the exceptional child.

Improving child education is emphasised in chapter five. Some of the topics considered are curriculum, career opportunities, teachers' roles, and teaching methods.

Chapter six deals with social vices and violence. It defined child abuse as well as discusses causes of child abuse and how to stop child abuse. It examines child labour, street hawking, effects of child labour on the child, drug abuse, cult, prostitution, gender violence and examination malpractice.

Chapter seven examines philosophy and policy formulation. Some of our educational problems such as non-implementation, non-availability of facilities and equipment, financial problems, inconsistency in education policy and day/boarding schools are considered.

In chapter eight, equipment and materials for schools are considered. The chapter offers some purchasing guidelines as well as community resources and recreational facilities for our schools.

Chapter nine deals with financing and budgeting. It takes a look at the Education Tax Decree No. 7 of 1993, educational vouchers as well as how to make education money go round.

Finally, chapter ten asks the question, what sort of future? Among other issues, it also examines the implications of vision 2010 on education.

ACKNOWLEDGEMENTS

I would like to acknowledge the contributions of friends, relations, and colleagues, too many to mention here in the preparation of this book.

In particular, I remain very grateful to my unique husband, Alhaji Atiku Abubakar, for his constant support, encouragement, as well as usual brotherly advice. His immense contributions led to the realisation of this book.

My gratitude also goes to Ali Ahmadu, Ex. Director of Finance, Education Tax Fund, Abuja, as well as Paul Muoh, Chief Executive, ACB General Nigeria Ltd., Kaduna and Public Relations Manager, Salini Nigeria Ltd., Abuja, for their tremendous encouragement and immense contributions.

To Dr. J. C. Ikerionwu, Head of Department of Counselling and Science Education, University of Abuja, Abuja, I say thank you for your scholarly suggestions. I am also grateful to Dr. J. Y. Maisamari, Director of Consultancy Services Unit, University of Abuja and Dr. J. B. Badu of the same university for their contributions.

Finally, the highest glory goes to the Almighty who has made the production of this book possible.

Chapter One

EDUCATION AND PHILOSOPHY

What is Education

It is important that all who play a part in the work of schools should remember that education existed long before organised schools or school teachers were ever thought of. Education is not something different from life and society, but is in fact that process of learning to live as a useful and acceptable member of the community. It is important also to realise that formal education, as provided in schools, is one of the least permanent of the forces which influence boys and girls.

The other conflicting social pressures of the community often quickly and permanently swallow up its effects. In times past, the community accepted and supported traditional forms of education as provided by parents in the home, and by priests in religious ceremonies or initiation rites, because this was in harmony with the traditions as a whole. Today, unfortunately, there is often a rift between schools and the community, because what the school offers has often very little in common with the standards and needs of the local community.

It is what makes the young primary school leaver who cannot find a job such a problem to himself, his family and community. The whole position is further confused by the modern trend of urbanisation and industrialisation, which brings together groups of people with different ways of life, standards of conduct, interests and beliefs. The teacher must see himself and his children as part of education in its widest sense, otherwise, his view will be short-sighted and his contribution will fall far short of what is needed. He must realise that educational aims may be immediate or long term, and that they may be social or individual.

Immediate goals are usually fairly easy to achieve, but are of little value apart from long-term aims. For example, a teacher may achieve quickly the immediate aim of making a child able to read words. But this is an insignificant aim compared with teaching a child to enjoy reading. On the social plane, there is no value in producing a child, who is good at his schoolwork, who is at the same time rebellious towards the community. All the aims of education should harmonise in seeking to produce people who are completely integrated with the community.

The social misfits, as well as the young school failure are both reflections of enriched goals of education. Too many teachers consider only their immediate aims and fail to ponder the long-term aims that alone make their efforts worthwhile. Usually, this is because the immediate problems seem more pressing. By ignoring the long term aims, teachers sacrifice the ultimate value of all their efforts, but by giving thought to them, they can enrich their lives and teaching, and make purposeful their work and their lessons.

What is Man?

Since education in its widest sense is learning to live, it is obvious that the nature of man and the purpose of life must be vital to a true understanding of the purpose of education. But immediately we ask such questions like "what is man?" or "what is the meaning of life?" We are swept into the ranks of philosophers, whose answers to such questions are legion. Basically, however, there are two answers. There are those who claim that all life is given by God, thus, to them, the purpose of man's life lies in the will and purpose of God. Others, who do not believe in God, regard the existence of man as the result of a process of evolution from chemical substances through lowly forms of life to man himself.

Each of these views has a profound effect upon those who hold them, and indeed they have influenced the course of history. But the classification is not a simple clear-cut one. Those who hold one view may range widely in the details of their philosophy.

For example, the first or religious view embraces the Christians, the

Muslims and the Animists; and the second or rationalist view includes such diverging groups as the humanists and the communists. But even when we have classified people in these ways, we have to acknowledge that within the religious groups, there are rationalists and amongst the rationalists, there are some who are deeply religious.

The ultimate dividing line is between those who take the revelation of God and the word of God as the final authority over man and his conduct, and those who put man himself as bearing the authority and responsibility for his life and development. Most rationalists are willing to accept anything that can be proved. But proof for them means tangible proof. They believe only in the world that they can see and measure, and in the natural laws, which they see controlling it. They see man as having come into existence by these inexorable laws and describe his origin in terms like evolution and natural selection.

To those who see man's existence in this way, mankind consist of individuals who are born into the world, live out their days, and go into oblivion at death. The value of each individual depends entirely on what he achieves in his lifetime, whether it be improving the state of society or merely passing on his knowledge to his children.

These views bring very different results. In the case of the humanists, a man is seen to be of intrinsic worth because of his thought, knowledge and intelligence. He is therefore worthy of respect as an individual in his own right. The communists, on the other hand, interpret the role of the individual as a log in the machine. For them, each man exists for the sake of the society. He bears the same relationship to society as the individual and also does to the nest to which he belongs.

In terms of history, both the humanists and communists regard each individual as contributing his services to a machine whether we call it civilisation or the sate. But though this contribution may be small, both are convinced that man, given time, can bring about a perfect society.

The religious groups are not so sure. They take into consideration not only man and his limited world space, time and material existence, but also his relationship to a supernatural world governed by God, its creator. They see themselves and their fellow men as the creatures of God and therefore subject to His divine will.

Life for them is a preparation for a future existence, which will be perfect. Their aim, therefore, in this life is to fulfil all that is required by the Creator to enter into His perfect kingdom. This sense of personal and physical involvement with a spiritual world reaching beyond the bounds of space and time is a fundamental difference between the religious view and the rationalist, it has a deep influence upon teachers who approach their work from different view points.

For example, the concept of a value like freedom varies according to one's philosophy. One rationalist view is that sometimes, it may be desirable for an individual to enjoy freedom but at other times it is not. It all depends on circumstances.

Another rationalist, on the other hand, thinks of freedom as a relative term, being absolute only when society is perfect. In the meantime, man must relinquish part of his freedom to the rule of whatever power he thinks is likely to bring about the greatest measure of freedom for all.

The religious view of freedom is that God gives to all men freedom to choose the kind of freedom they want. It concedes with the other philosophies that freedom is good only when the individual is willing to give up his freedom to do as he likes and subjects himself to authority and law. To do otherwise is to bring about anarchy. But with the religious view, perfect freedom is enjoyed when the individual freely chooses to yield up his freedom and make himself subject to God.

Man's understanding of democracy and authority, equality and inequality, love and demand, duty and pleasure, all depend on his personal philosophy concerning the nature and destiny of man.

That is why you, as a teacher must ponder these things so that your teaching may be purposeful and with conviction. Nothing is more out of keeping with principles of education than the teacher who holds certain values and seeks to share them with others without knowing why he holds them or understanding what their full meaning is.

What is Truth?

In a world in which ideologies conflict and lead ever more closely to the threat of global, atomic war and the annihilation of man, it is reasonable to ask, "What in the world is real and what is illusory? What is true and what is false? What is good and what is evil?"

Philosophers have asked the same questions from early times but reached different conclusions. One has said in answer to the question on whether man is real or not, "I believe I exist". Others, uncertain of any reality beyond the present material world, have set down the code for life "Let us eat, drink and be merry, for tomorrow we will die". These are all rationalist views.

The religious view rejects the rationalist philosophy as man-made and sees God as the source of all reality and all truth. In this view, history and eternity are married and reality is defined as a revealed truth.

The root trouble with society is that it is not sure of the reality or the value of its individuals. Side by side with modern technological progress, there has been a remarkable decline in conviction concerning ultimate reality and purposes. In this process, the machine has replaced the individual not only in his work, but in his status.

The nuclear bomb and the rocket have diverted the concern of man from man himself and turned him into a refugee of his own creation. Society is in danger of developing the wretched morale of a refugee camp. It is for this reason that teachers must take stock of what is real and true and good.

But how are we to know these values? If we inquire what men mean by good, we find there is not much agreement as might be expected. Instead, we find goodness tends to be simply what is regarded as good in one's own community. Thus, there are communities in the world where effeminacy among men, building or success on crime and other characteristics, widely held in other communities as repulsive, are regarded with approval as being good.

The fact that there are perhaps isolated cases or minorities among mankind does not lessen the argument that goodness is thought by most people, not as an absolute standard, but rather in an empirical or relative sense in that it is what suits our need. It is rather like the way we use the word "good" about a bicycle or sewing machine when they serve our needs well. They cease to be good when they break down and no longer do their job.

The same applies to truth. Throughout history, men have sought to find the truth about their world, the laws that govern it and their own existence. But again, we see the same pattern of divergent opinions in which some believe man's present state to be the climax of an incredibly long period of development, whereas, others hold to a belief in the creation of man at some fixed point of time. None of these views can be proved scientifically.

There always comes a point where the mind must take a step of faith. The danger to truth is when men find pleasure in the machinery of the search for it. When this happens, their concentration moves to the fascination of a game with words and ideas, and sight is lost of the real purpose of their search.

The rationalist takes his step of faith by placing his faith in his own reason and so truth for him becomes what he says it is. The religious view takes a step of faith, which opens up communication between God and man. The obvious problem, when we consider the varied rationalist interpretations of truth and the differences amongst those who hold a religious view of truth is "who is right?" If all the rationalist has to do is to argue convincingly, and all the holder of religious views has to do is to plead that God has spoken to him, are we any nearer to the truth if we listen to them?

The answer is "yes" if they keep on getting the same honest answer from their search. If any single rationalist philosophy is true, it will always reach the same answer. Its proof will always lead to the same conclusions. Likewise, if any religious view of truth is right, it will always teach the same truths. Any religious view of God must regard God as absolute and unchanging truth.

Thus, any religious view, which claims a changing record of revealed truth, must be suspected of being influenced more by man with his changing values and standards than by an unchanging God. This can be our only test of truth.

Today, because so many people holding rationalist and religious views of truth find themselves holding conceptions of truth, which are relative and not absolute, we find all kinds of values in a state of flux. Moral standards are losing their absolute qualities and traditional codes of behaviour are becoming quickly outdated because they do not make sense in the modern world.

The distinction between right and wrong is becoming hazy. The result is a society that lacks a sense of security and this society is fathering a new society in which the original concepts of truth and goodness will be almost meaningless. What can the teacher who fears the demoralisation of society do? Should he push his views down the throat of his pupils? This would be to deny the children individual freedom and breed an intense sectarian form of education. Reaction to this would bring about an opposite effect to that intended; this is seen in the American system of state education where, today, religious instruction is forbidden although the whole system was founded in a country in which religious beliefs were once deeply felt.

The teacher should present his beliefs in action, not as a classroom subject, but through his life. That is not to say that formal teaching will have no place. On the contrary, truth cannot be found in ignorance; it can only be understood and interpreted in terms of what we know. But the proof of truth will be evident as something more than a mere philosophy.

It will be demonstrated as a working and satisfying way of life, which the child is free to choose or reject. By this, the teacher shows he respects the freedom and individuality of personal choice, while offering the best life he knows to those he teaches.

Importance of Education to the Nigerian Child

Getting Orientated (Tasks for Child Education)
If we ask different kinds of people what they think about the importance of child education, we will be surprised and perhaps confused by the diversity of their answers and the conflicting aims expressed. Employers tend to look for skill and character, politicians for members and gratifying statistics, religious leaders for spiritual quality, while parents are content only with success.

If you ask them what is wrong with education, some will point to the schools, some, the curriculum and some will accuse the teachers who, no doubt, will pass the blame onto the children and "this modern generation". Most people have plenty to say about the importance of child education and are willing to offer opinion on what should be done, but few venture to say why.

Government opinion is notoriously short sighted. This makes it all the more important for the Ministry of Education to sit down and think what its real tasks are and why they need to be done.

The aim of child education can best be expressed as a series of tasks which must be fulfilled. They cannot be accomplished overnight. They will take time, for they are not immediate goals. Rather, they are tasks which give meaning to the vast amount of machinery that has to be built up in the name of educating the Nigerian Child and being so widely misused.

When these tasks are tackled with understanding, they give purpose to the energy of those thousands of men and women who have chosen a career in improving the Education of the Nigerian child. These tasks are not the ultimate goal of child education. The truth is, each person must fend for himself.

Passing on the Heritage of the Past
When the child is born, he begins a new personal existence, but he also joins an old established society. One of the tasks of the country, the parents and the society is to pass knowledge to him. The child who finishes secondary school today knows more general science than Newton did and more geography than Columbus.

He can learn more in school about the atom or the aeroplane than his grandfather could have learned at a university. In few years at school, he learns the mathematics that has taken man some thousands of years to develop.

If he becomes a scientist, he will have the unusual experience of knowing that his generation lived, indeed, with ever developing techniques in preparation for space travel and colonisation of other planets, we as a nation may be teaching the last generation of children who are wholly earth bound.

But the child is deeply indebted to past generations for all those discoveries and the accumulated experience that have been handed down to him. Civilisation as we know it, would cease to exist if ever the heritage of the past were withheld from the present children. This heritage is not only national but also international, and it concerns not only the present, but also the future.

In the past, this heritage was passed on through the family or by contact between individuals. Today, the increased quantity of knowledge and greater numbers of people acquiring it require a good school system of child education as a foundation.

Who knows whether this will meet the needs of the future? A good child education must meet the need of the present, yet keep its eye always on the future. The importance of child education for today is a maxim which has deep undertones of meaning.

There is therefore no ideal type of child education suitable for all times. It is always a tragedy, when a form of education developed for a place and time in the past is used somewhere else in the present. Examples of this are found in some parts of Africa, where a European pattern of school and curriculum is followed in a way, which makes them quite inappropriate to Africa and the modern scene.

Children education in this way finds it difficult to be assimilated into the community, whether we are thinking of the states, area councils and the nations as a whole. Inevitably, if they are to be fully integrated with their own community, they must make adjustments at the points where education failed to have relevance to the needs and aspiration of their community.

Throughout the world, education must achieve a reintegration of the school child with his community, otherwise the disintegration of the community is bound to follow, but it can only happen if throughout his education, he is constantly made to feel himself a part of the community. Obviously, these requirements will necessitate some rethinking concerning the curriculum and the organisation of many schools.

Passing on the heritage of the past assumes that we are anticipating a future, which in turn assumes that we can survive. Some civilisations of the past have been completely extinguished through war, famine or disease. Education thus has a task, which is a prerequisite to passing on the heritage of the past that is teaching the young child how to live in the future generation in which they will be adults.

Preparing for the Future

In the most primitive state of man's whole preoccupation, he is concerned with keeping alive. This involves doing the right thing for his gods, his family and his work. The correct sacrifices must be offered lest the anger of his gods should destroy him. This is tied up with his fear of human and natural enemies, which constantly endanger his life. The duties and the relationships within the family must be accepted by all its members because the family is dependent on itself as a unit for survival. To avoid starvation, the man must become a master of the skills required to obtain his food whether it be through hunting or farming.

This pattern of religion, society and bread winning activity is repeated in modern society, but is immensely more complicated. It is not possible for every man to know everything. Specialisation becomes necessary. Thus we have Priests, Imams and those engaged full time in the religious aspect of life. We have soldiers to protect us from human enemies, doctors to protect us from diseases and so forth.

We no longer supply our food entirely from what we grow; instead, we sell our labour and buy our food with the proceeds. Bread wining therefore depends on our having skill in the kind of labour which are needed by the country. It is possible for you to be a graduate of a university, but if what you have to offer the community is not what it wants, you will surely starve to death; unless you are prepared to adapt or move to another community that can use your skill.

To prepare children for living in the modern world, the nation must provide something of the threefold quality of ancient education, but apply it to the specialisation of our times. The merits of each emphasis can be debated, though many people believe that school ought not to specialise but take each with equal emphasis. Certainly in the primary school it would be a mistake to specialise. Good living must be presented as a harmony of the spirit, the mind and the body. Healthy habits of conduct must be instilled, worthwhile skills taught and healthy activities of the mind encouraged, not just so that the children may be prepared for earning a living or for exercising their intellect, but rather for coping with the problems of the community of which they will soon find themselves adult members.

Putting Purpose into Life

For many people, both young and old, life is without real purpose. Routine tasks are repeated day after day. They meet and work with the same people. They talk about the same thing. The pattern of life is repetitive and colourless. Consequently, they seek to escape from it and they do so in various ways. The trouble is that they see nothing in the purpose of life that they value greatly or feel is worth starving for. Thus the adding of knowledge, instead of bringing greater satisfaction, brings increased frustration because it serves no purpose.

The modern world has no single embracing view of life. Knowledge is studied in the watertight compartments of subjects; scholars learn more and more about less and less. Man himself ceases to be an individual with a destiny and becomes an organism with an anatomy and a mind with complexes.

The more complete this divorce becomes between life and destiny, knowledge and purpose, what and why, the more difficult it becomes to achieve reconciliation between them. But if education means anything, such reconciliation must be made and the obvious place for it to start is in the hearts of the children, from the lowliest kindergarten, primary school, and teachers to the leading university professors.

The problem is intimately related to what we considered in the details on education and philosophy. But our thoughts on these must not end merely in a mental exercise, they must end in a philosophy of life, which we lived firmly because it gives a satisfying purpose of all we learn and do. Maybe we will call it duty, maybe pleasure, maybe something else, but it will keep us from living lives that are aimless. It will help us to show the children we teach, that our labours in teaching them and their efforts in learning are for a better purpose than making them skilled in mental gymnastics; for they will, in fact, help them to become men and women of real understanding.

Without a philosophy of education you will be swayed by the most recent fashions in teaching, and become absorbed with the means to the end more than the end itself. You will fail to convince your children that life has purpose and education is worthwhile. Unless you succeed in making the education you provide something that influences the very life of the child, you may well have the bitter disappointment of seeing your children throw off their education like an unwanted garment when they leave school, and you may well ask yourself then, thinking of all your wasted effort, "was it worth it?"

Government

The desired improvement on early childhood education in Nigeria starts with the government, if prevailing circumstances, such as underdevelopment of children are taken into consideration. A child develops most, mentally and physically, at pre-primary and primary school levels. Hence, the saying, "catch a child at three and you catch him forever." The future growth of the nation's economy is hinged on sound development of the leaders of tomorrow - the children.

The government then has an important role as guardian, through formulating and implementing a comprehensive National Policy on Education. Education is a highly complex industry that requires its production lines to work in harmony, effectively, and efficiently. Any imbalance in one aspect of the system will ultimately throw the whole mechanism out of order.

Consequently, the improvement on pre-primary and primary education can be done more fruitfully in the context of the entire educational system. Government should, before formulating any educational policy, plan a purposeful education with an eye on the economy of the country. With proper planning, government should be able to establish the right kind of education required to foster national development.

Government should realise that education should be guided by the following principles:

- Democratisation of education; a concept tied to that of social justice, which is the major idea of our time;
- Development of all aspects of the human personality through an education that not only provides knowledge but creates personalities who use their knowledge in action.
- A culture that is humanist, scientific and technical, and which brings out the relationship between humanism and technology.

Therefore, in formulating a National Policy on Education, with pre-primary and primary education as the foundation, the government acting as a control unit, should:

1. Set standard for required quality of teachers, in terms of building structure, which has to be uniformed; a uniform curriculum;

instructional materials/equipment; facilities, especially library, minimum and maximum population per classroom.

2. Recognise the development of the handicapped and gifted children by means of providing special schools, instructional materials and equipment for their learning and development.

3. Provide better incentive to motivate willing citizens to go into the teaching profession. In addition, see to the overall welfare of teachers — paying salaries promptly on schedule, loan schemes (car, furniture and housing), etc.

4. Provide a policy, which will emphasise on skill, science and technology by establishing secondary, technical and vocational schools of well-equipped standard.

5. Set up appropriate uniform mechanisms to solve the problems of funding and management at all level of education.

6. Train specialised teachers in secondary, technical, vocational, special (handicapped and gifted) schools in methods of teaching in various colleges of education and universities.

Recommendations

The following recommendations are suggested:

1. Public and private schools should meet the standard set by the government for uniformed and harmonised learning process and condition.
2. For the health and safety of the children, an up-to-date certificate of immunization and physical health examination should be required to enrol a child. Equally, insurance policy should be taken to protect every child on playground injury.

3. The training of teachers in sociology, psychology, philosophy, and psychiatry is of utmost importance and should be made compulsory in the curriculum of colleges of education and universities. This is

to enable teachers identify children, who are better at certain skills than others and therefore group them and help gear them toward their skills. It will help for placement in the right school.

4. There is an urgent need to provide avenues for the upgrading and professional development of practising teachers of the pre-primary, primary and secondary school levels, which should be embarked upon so that they would be able to face the challenges of the "New National Policy on Education".

5. Teachers should be encouraged to teach in the rural areas by providing basic amenities in those areas such as low cost housing schemes and paying them higher salary which will serve as bonus for the teachers there to encourage and motivate them.

REFERENCES

Adaralegbe, A. 1772. *A Philosophy for Nigerian Education.* Report of the National Curriculum Conference, Sept. 8-12, 1969. Lagos: NERDC.

Dewey, J. 1916. *Democracy and Education.* New York: Macmillan.

Driscoll, F. 1972. "Transcendental Meditation as a Secondary School Subject." *Phi Delta Kappan* (December).

Fafunwa, A.B. 1974. *History of Education in Nigeria.* London: George Allen & Unwin.

Federal Republic of Nigeria. 1998. *National Policy on Education.* Lagos: NERDC Press.

Kneller, G.E. 1974. *Introduction to the Philosophy of Education.* New York: John Wiley and Sons.

Obinidike, O.E. 1980. *The Foundations of Philosophy of Education.* Jos: University Press.

Okafor, F.C. 1981. *Philosophy of Education and Third World Perspectives.* Lawrenceville, Virginia: Brunswick Publishing Co.

Royce, J.R. 1964. *The Encapsulated Man.* New York: D.Van Nostrand Company.

Thakur, A.S. 1976. *The Philosophical Foundations of Education.* Zaria: ABU Press.

Udo, E. 1969. "Teacher education." In Adaralegbe, A. (1972). (ed.). *A Philosophy for Nigerian Education.* Lagos: NERDC.

Zais, R.S. 1976. *Curriculum: Principles and Foundations.* New York: Harper & Row, Publishers.

Chapter Two

NIGERIA AND THE RIGHTS OF THE CHILD

The Rights of the Child

A child is any human being below the age of 18, his/her right is a natural due, a moral claim, and a legal entitlement. If we then talk of children's rights, we are talking of child survival, development and participation in social, political, and economical activities of the society.

Some of the basic principles of children's rights are the right to live, survive and develop; the right to a name, family and nationality; freedom to belong to any association or assembly according to the law; the right to express opinions and freely communicate on any issue subject to restriction under the law; entitlement to protection from any act that interferes with his or her privacy, honour, and reputation; the right to adequate rest, recreation (leisure and play) according to his or her age and culture; the right to receive compulsory basic education and equal opportunity for higher education depending on individual ability; the right to have good health, protection from illness and proper medical attention for survival, personal growth and development.

The right to be protected from indecent and inhuman treatment through sexual exploitation, drug abuse, child labour, torture, maltreatment and neglect; the right not to suffer any discrimination irrespective of ethnic, origin, birth, colour, sex, language, religion, political and social beliefs, status or disability.

The parents and government have the duty to protect and respect these rights of the child. In like manner they have to encourage programmes, activities and policies that promote the expression, participation and defence of these rights by the child. On the part of the child, he or she must not see these rights as opportunities to engage in misconduct and injurious activities that can jeopardise his/her or others' chances of development and survival.

The child too has some responsibilities to shoulder, such as respecting his superiors, parents and elders; to contribute to the well being of the society, morally by preserving and strengthening the social and national integrity; upholding the cultural values of the society.

Conventions on the Rights of the Child

The rights of the child were adopted by the General Assembly of the United Nations on November 20, 1989.

Preambles

The preambles recall the basic principles of the United Nations and specific provisions of certain relevant human rights treaties and proclamations. They reaffirm the fact that children, because of their vulnerability, need special care and protection. They place special emphasis on the primary caring and protective responsibility of the family. They also reaffirm the needs for legal and other protection of the child before and after birth, the importance of respect for the cultural values of the child's community, and the vital role of international co-operation in securing children's right.

The General Assembly of the United Nations adopted a total of forty-two articles on November 20, 1989. Some of the articles that pertain to education are:

Article 1: Definition of a child. A child is recognised as a person under 18, unless national laws recognise the age of majority earlier.

Article 12: The child's opinion. The child has the right to express his or her opinion freely and to have that opinion taken into account in any matter or procedure affecting the child.

Article 13: Freedom of expression. The child has the right to express his or her views, obtain information, and make ideas or information known, regardless of frontiers.

Article 28: Education. The child has a right to education, and the states duty is to ensure that primary education is free and compulsory, to encourage different forms of secondary education accessible to every child and to make higher education available to all on the basis of capacity. School discipline shall be consistent with the child's rights and dignity. The state shall engage in international co-operation to implement this right.

Article 28: Aims of education. Education shall aim at developing the child personality, talents and mental and physical abilities to the fullest. Education shall prepare the child for an active adult life in a free society and foster respect for the child's parents, his or her own cultural identity, language and values of theirs.

Child Study

In education, scientific child study is comparatively recent. Formerly children were regarded often as if they were miniature adult and, because of this, both the matter and the methods of their teaching were often unsuitable. But child study has shown that growing up is more than growing bigger.

A poet once said, "The child is father of the man". By this he meant that the grown man is the outcome of development begun in childhood. If this development is controlled and directed, then the kind of adults in our future society can in some good measure be determined.

Just as in the medical profession, the student doctor must learn all he can about the human body, its component parts, how they grow, how they work, what goes wrong with them and how their diseases can be cured. So the teacher today must realise the importance of studying children and the factors which affect their development.

Child study may be undertaken in a specialised capacity but the average teacher is not likely to have the time to become an expert in any of its branches such as psychology, psychiatry, social welfare or paediatrics. Most of what he needs to know can be gotten from interest in, and intelligent observation of children. Observation is the key to child study.

Your knowledge should not come therefore primarily from books about children, but from children themselves. This child study for the student in training school should be a practical matter in which plenty opportunity is given for observation and experience in dealing with children.

One of the first things you notice when you study children is how different they are from each other and how each develops at his or her own pace along his or her own path of progress. There is therefore no such thing as the typical child. Child study can also help us to diagnose and suggest treatment for children who, for some reason vary considerably from normal.

But it is only when we know what to expect from the normal child that this becomes a possibility. Thus, the study of normal development is fundamental to child study and it is the aspect you should always concentrate on.

There are some methods of child study. Experience has shown that the best way of collecting information about children, so that valid comparisons between different children can be made, is the questionnaire. But the kind of questionnaire you need and the way you use it depends very much on the purpose of your study. For instance, if you want to find out what the average child of a certain age is like, you will have to set questions to a very large number of children of this age.

The questions will have to cover the various lines along which children progress, such as physical, mental, emotional and social development. This task is to be done by the teacher. However, by using smaller samples, some ideas of the typical Nigerian child at different ages can be gained.

In addition to questionnaires, child study makes use of various tests such as:

a. Intelligence tests which try to relate the mental ability of an individual child to the "norm" for his or her age.
b. Attainment tests which examine what the child has achieved in learning. They are used for assessing progress in school subjects.
c. Diagnostic tests which try to find the specific weaknesses in a child's performance in school subjects.

d. Personality tests which try to assess the emotional and social maturity of the child.

In Nigeria it is difficult to get standardised tests of these kinds. But the important thing for us to do is to be aware of the differences in intelligence, attainment and personality, and take steps to develop special abilities and cure weaknesses of the children. What we need to do is to keep our eyes, ears and mind open, so that we do not miss opportunities to give help where and when it is needed.

The teacher should understand that there is no such thing as "normal" child, such is simply an imaginary child in whom all the characteristics usually found in children of his or her age have been collected. But in child study the term "normal" could be used in qualifying a child who has met certain accepted characteristics.

It is important to understand how the differences amongst children come about, so that you are able to give help to the unusual child in the problems that he or she faces because of his or her unusual qualities, and it will also help you to allow the normal child to progress at his or her best speed.

Each of us grows up under the two important influences of heredity and environment. Heredity gives us our inborn and often latent talents, our physical and mental mechanism with all its strength and weaknesses. Environment, like the blacksmith's forge, tempers and alters our natural characteristics according to the treatment given.

Each newborn child is a unique creation, different in detail from any other. Nevertheless, heredity makes each of us similar to our fellow men and most like our relatives. Environment moulds and alters us, sometimes making us more like each other and sometimes exaggerating our differences. The interplay of heredity and environment is responsible for nearly all the close likenesses and wide differences to be found amongst human beings — children.

Psychologists have always been keen to discover just what proportion of our make-up is due to heredity and what to environment. But they have never been able to decide. Probably the truth is that the ratio is different in each one of us. In some, heredity dominates the life and behaviour of the individual; in others it is environment.

The stronger and more dominant the forces of either heredity or environment are, the greater are their effects on the individual. In our development, the individual's choice on how to respond to our environment makes the conscious human behaviour unpredictable. This you will find differently amongst children.

Too often in child study, we are tempted to over-concentrate on certain aspects of the child's make-up and fail to see him or her as a whole. The wholeness of the child is evident at birth when the stimulation of one part of his or her body brings his or her whole body into action. This is a result of a well co-ordinated relationship that binds together the spirit, mind and body. The child is never quite in equilibrium as he or she responds to the environment according to the reaction of the whole body. This is important because, in training the child, we must put into consideration these three aspects of any human being. We must deal with the whole child (spirit, mind and body). The teacher must appreciate the fact that education must deal with the child in this sense if it is to help him or her grow into a healthy, well-balanced adult.

What we call growing up is not a smooth process of development but rather a series of periods of progress spaced with periods of rest. His or her rests allow very necessary consolidation to take place. Rapid growth in one direction must always be followed by consolidation. The development of the child can be thought of as four parallel processes; physical, mental, emotional and social. But these are not separate and independent processes. Each react with others and each makes possible the development of the others. The child is a whole.

Innate Tendencies of Man

Man's innate tendencies or inner propensities are used to describe those varied patterns of behaviour, which he reveals and which help him and his species to survive. Psychologists are not agreed as to whether these tendencies are actually inherited or whether they are patterned by our social environment throughout childhood. Suffice it to say, that the tendencies are quite marked and some are of particular importance to the teacher.

It would be wrong to think of man's behaviour as the product of these tendencies. Rather, these tendencies are the ways in which his life is expressed. Man has a will to live and this will to live expresses itself in the innate tendencies. The will to live expresses itself in two main tendencies from which stem all the others. These are the urge to give and the urge to get.

The urge to give shows itself in the creativeness which is seen at an early age in children and which continues through adult life, expressed in different ways in the home, in business, art, social work and social relations. The urge, controlled and used for the good of humanity, is capable of giving to the nation the grandest and most sublime contributions of man to art and science. But, alas, we also found the urge perverted when our getting turns to theft, or collecting to miserliness and our search for happiness to rape and self-gratification.

In human beings, the deepest satisfaction is found in those acts where giving is offered freely, without hope of reward, but is in fact recompensed. This is the pleasure enjoyed when praise or thanks is returned for a service gladly given or when the respect and love shown by one individual to another is mutual.

Circumstances of environment may prevent the growth of these urges into positive action or cause their power to be directed to bad ends. The teacher's aim should be to encourage and utilise these powerful forces that lie within each of our children and so channel them, that their influence may be directed towards all that is good and worthwhile and away from what is evil. This will improve not only the children's characters, but will aid them in their learning and the teachers in their teaching.

The innate tendencies of man, which are of importance to education, are listed in Table 2.1 together with their usual modes of expression.

Table 2.1: The Innate Tendencies of Man and Usual Mode of Expression

INNATE TENDENCY	USUAL MODE OF EXPRESSION
Creativeness	Building, constructing, modelling, assembling, selecting, arranging, pattern making, shaping, inventing
Collecting	Making collections of material things or accumulating abstract but measurable qualities like knowledge, power, etc., all of which either give pleasure, are useful, valuable, or likely to impress somebody else

Curiosity	Wandering, investigation, experimenting, wondering
Gregariousness	Seeking out and enjoying the company of others, making friends, finding pleasure in teamwork and doing things with others
Self Assertion	Leadership, pride, asserting, independence, ambition, teasing, aggressiveness, bullying, attack
Self Submission	Obedience and devotion to another person, respectfulness, humility, shyness
Self Preservation	Running away from danger, fear and anger when frustrated or interfered with
Play	Performing activities which exercise physical and mental skills, imitating people or things either seriously or in make-belief, making use of objects, toys, and materials in the furtherance of play

Behaviour of the Child

Behaviour comes in many forms and it is constant. It is good and bad, sometimes natural. Children's behaviours may be influenced by cultural differences as will a teacher's attitude to acceptance and non-acceptance of certain behaviours.

Some notable behaviours among children are: the habit of saying "thank you", sharing, giggles, smiles, quiet play, boisterous pushing and shoving, fussiness, whining, foul language, back-talk, bickering, fist fights, kicking, hair pulling, pinching, biting, lying, jealousy, anger and stealing.

Sometimes you find a child being involved in one or some of these behaviours. At times, it is an ugly and risky behaviour, destructive actions, moody behaviour, and at other times, it could be a pleasant one full of love and affection.

This is all the world of children the teacher ought to study carefully to have a clear understanding on how to teach them to learn better. Although teachers and parents must remain "in charge", children should be encouraged to participate in discussions, express ideas and make choices. If you desire the well-being of the child, then he or she must participate to create mutual understanding.

What to do as a Teacher and When

A teacher should know what to do and when to do it, whenever a child exhibits one of these behaviours whether good, bad or natural. This will enable the teacher tolerate and handle the situation without psychologically hurting the child's emotion, or making him or her weak in discharging her duty.

Children always need time to obey, and an advance notice of the close of an activity to adjust to the idea of stopping the activity is necessary. This will help check frustration and anger in the child. Whenever there is any disturbing behaviour during an activity or in a situation, children should not be allowed to go back to such activity or situation. Children have no sense of time and the length of time really has no connection with the disruptive behaviour.

Teach children how to share with one another to avoid boisterous behaviour. Crying and tantrums are not the most pleasant aspects of life, but apparent ignorance of the behaviour seems to work sometimes so long as you keep an eye on the child. Tiredness, hunger or sickness may cause fussiness in a child which could be taken care of with a snack or ask the child to run round the playground, if the child is five years and above.

Children learn foul language quickly as they hear and use it. To such behaviour, explain to the child that such language is not good to be used. Notify the child's parents and try to identify the source from which the child has learned the foul language. If the source is controlled, the language should cease.

Parental influence is so interwoven with the school behaviour of children that teachers must have parents' goodwill and help in planning and carrying through with behaviour development. Parents and teachers relationship is essential in children's behaviour control or management.

To children of three, four and five-year-old, back talk such as "no, I don't have to" is normal. But this can be eased by ignoring the child's behaviour, not answering any conversation that contains the back talk. In extreme cases, isolate the child from the situation with a firm reminder that you do not accept the behaviour.

Do not get into an oral confrontation with the child; you may get more back talk. Some children get loved when they are in the group of the same children for longer time, then bickering occurs. With adequate planning, activities should change at very short intervals, say 20 minutes, with different groups of children.

Fist-fights may happen for various reasons and are usually spontaneous and short-lived. Whenever these occur, put the participants in different areas apart. Later, discuss with the children why fighting is wrong and give them alternatives.

Children who are kickers, pinchers, hair pullers and biters do these when they are playing with others or when being hunted in their behaviour by adults. This behaviour is not unusual. Put the attackers in the quiet corner in such a case.

Frequent tantrums are a sign of a very tired, neglected, or spoiled child. A child who is tired just cannot handle any more activities, and a neglected child just need proper attention. A spoilt child who uses tantrum to get whatever he or she wants is a serious problem. In this case, ignore the child but with careful watching eyes.

Children may lie because they have done something they know they will be punished for, they are trying to cope with a problem, or they don't remember what happened. Generally, if teachers are responsible in their expectations of young children and in their type of punishment, children will not lie. Children become very imaginative when they have problems. So, when you know the tale cannot possibly be true, look for the cause. You do not need to accuse the child of lying because he or she knows it.

Children are very sensitive to unfairness, lack of attention or classroom favouritism, which always lead to jealousy. Those children who are more jealous than others can be helped by making them helpers for other children. Stealing doesn't occur very often but when it does, the culprit may be hard to find. Any purposeful stealing, when discovered, needs to be punished.

Some problems of behaviour happen once and never again, while some may occur over and over again. Children differ in social and emotional development just as they do in physical and intellectual development. Spanking or hitting the child does not help matters in handling the unwanted behaviour of the child. This could inflict emotional injuries to children and cause them to become defiant in the future.

If unacceptable behaviour continues, and all possible solutions are applied, including parents' involvement, the child may be excused from school for some time with an explanation to the parent(s). Don't tell the child he or she is bad or mean, or that you don't love him or her. Just say the child forgot how to behave well.

A research finding, conducted by Ronald Drabman and Margaret Hanratty Thomas on the influence of the conduct of TV actors on the behaviour of young children, shows how the behaviours of children are sometimes influenced by what they watch on TV. Watching television actually has become a way of life for children recently. Because of their inability to separate fact from fiction, they not only become placid about violence, they often model behaviour that appears to be silly, funny or dangerous. This behaviour can cause serious problems both in school and at home.

Non-verbal Behaviour
Teachers cannot rely only on listening skills to determine the feelings or behaviour of the children they teach. It is important that teachers also look into the non-verbal behaviour of children, which also transmit feelings and reaction. Children catch up non-verbal stimuli from their friends and adults equally. Their physical and verbal behaviour is often influenced by the non-verbal cues extended by the teacher. As a teacher, you need to study your non-verbal behaviour as well as the children's. You may be causing your own problems.

Some of the non-verbal behaviour cues are; facial expressions, gestures, eye contact and posture, biting tongue or lips, extended chest, extended lower lip, furrowed brow, smile, mouth twitch, frown, clenched fists, pale face, reflexes arm muscles, downcast eyes, limb arms, dropped head, gleam in eye, scowl, drooping mouth, rigid body, etc.

Manners
What are good manners for children? Learning to share toys and take turns are probably the first manners that young children have to learn. This is a long-term goal and has to be taught by example, fairness, and many different opportunities. This should be practised often to drive home the idea that everyone gives up something and everyone gets something. A timer is an inexpensive item for timing the play, for sharing and taking turns.

Table manners are other things the children can learn. Table manners should be observed on each occasion of eating. Children should be exposed to more of such eating occasions. These manners are taught and caught through practical experience. Only through practice and observation of good table manners can children learn the manners you want them to have.

Company manners are also learnt from example and are easier to teach when the children are younger. Greeting classroom guests by shaking their hands, taking their coats, seating them, and talking to them should be practised early. Children can practice by taking turns being guests. Invite guests (parent too) to visit and let the children do all the company manners taught them as a way of practice. Only through practice will children be comfortable with these social skills.

Manners must be identified, planned for, taught and demonstrated. Good manners should be shown daily by both the child and the teacher.

Praises

Catch the child being good! Praise is the oral language used to recognise right and positive behaviour. Oral encouragement can be given to their children before they begin a task, as they are doing it, or after they have finished it.

Teachers should know when to praise a child for behaving well, giving it quietly and at the appropriate time. Overused praise is not effective. Praise and attention should be spread to everyone in the classroom, but do not praise everyone for every activity unless they deserve it. Children should know which behaviour is being praised by the teacher's careful handling of it.

Praise words include: that's right, marvellous! Much better, good, great! Beautiful! Excellent! Good thinking. Terrific! Keep it up, that's really nice, congratulations!

Young children are greatly influenced by their teachers as well as their parents and peers. Therefore, a teacher must be an agent of change in some instances, a conveyor of behaviour at other times, and a model of consistent behaviour at all times. The realisation of how behaviour is acquired and knowledge of right behaviour, will make a good teacher better.

REFERENCES

Bronfenbrenner, U. 1970. *Two Worlds of Childhood.* New York: Russel Sage Foundation.

Dubey, D.L.; Dubey, O.E.C. and Ndagi, J.O. 1985. *Teaching in the Primary School.* London: Longman Group Ltd.

Goodman, L.V. 1976 "A Bill of Rights for the Handicapped." *American Education* 12:6-8.

Graubard, A. 1972. *Free the Children.* New York: Pantheon.

Onwuegbu, O.I. 1979. *Discover Teaching.* Enugu: Fourth Dimension Publishing Co.

Rogers, C. 1969. *Freedom to Learn.* Columbus: Charles E. Merwill.

Chapter Three

CHILD EDUCATION

Children need to feel loved and wanted. Try to respond in ways which shows that your pupils are cared for and prized. Children need to feel that they belong. So, try to respond in ways which are accepting and inviting. Children also need to feel successful, for this reason we should try to provide opportunities that ensure genuinely successful achievement. They need t6 equally feel secured and we should try to respond in ways which will not threaten or undermine their sense of well being.

Their need to be free from intense feelings of guilt has to be fulfilled by response in ways which attend to the feelings, and which do not shame or humiliate them. Children need to be free from intense feelings of fear. Our response in calming and reassuring ways, which do not ridicule children's fears, is what we should cultivate. They need to be respected too, which means we should try to respond in ways that show genuine interest in who they are and in what they think.

Early Childhood Education
Background information concerning programmes, teachers and careers is important for a basic understanding of what educating young children is all about. These factors also determine the quality as well as the quantity of opportunities for children. Some individuals thrive on the verbal and physical interaction that take place in any group of young children, while other individuals find the constant action too demanding both physically and mentally.

Early education needs are expanding yearly and the possibilities of establishing a lifelong pleasurable experience are many. Today, the majority of early education programmes serve a wide variety of purposes.

Parents wish for a variety of experience for their children, and because of the great influx of parents' involvement in activities in the school setting, the purposes of early education programmes by necessity may vary greatly even within the same city.

In traditional early childhood programme, opportunities for socialisation and creative activities were emphasised. In some instances, beginning reading and mathematics instruction was an important part of the day's programme. These aspects of early childhood programmes still dominate today's schools. Socialisation, creativity and an introduction to science, mathematics, social studies, art, music, physical development and reading are recognised as valid goals for all young children in early education programmes. A comparatively new concept in early childhood education was developed in the early 1960s.

The concept of early intervention began with a national comprehensive programme for disadvantaged children that were created as a part of the "War on Poverty". The studies of Bloom, Brunner and Hunt, among others, seem to confirm the importance of environmental factors in facilitating the development of children. Although, many experimental programmes exist, research findings to date seem to reinforce the earlier studies regarding the effectiveness of early intervention prior to kindergarten. A 1973 study reported that approximately 2.5 million children under the age of six come from poverty-level families where the mother does not work.

In addition to being economically disadvantaged, many of these children do not receive the environmental stimulation necessary for cognitive development. A recent 1980 study reported more positive gains than other studies have reported. It indicated that children who attended kindergarten scored higher in basic skills test than those who did not have kindergarten education. Those who attended kindergarten are likely not to fail.

Nature and Extent of Programmes

Among the extensive and varied programmes concerned with the total development of human potential, early childhood programmes are in the forefront. Any type of programme best for young children has a better chance of success if it is properly planned and administered; careful attention to the planning and administrative aspects of programmes for children can prevent costly, frivolous and counterproductive mistakes. The effectiveness of planning and administration begin with some perspective of the nature and extent of early childhood programmes. Briefly, some of the major programmes are as follows:

Day care

This generally refers to programmes that operate in extended houses and offer service for children of age three or younger, through school age. The day-care programmes involve the care and education of children who are separated from their parents for all or part of the day. The participation of women in the labour force has taken a dramatic upsurge during the last decade. Single mothers and partners in dual-career families have contributed to a change in the labour force that shows no signs of abating.

One consequence of this change has been to find alternative forms of care for children of working parents. This day care comes in various forms like on-site day care, which is located at the work-site by the employer (e.g. hospital, industry etc.). Off-site work-related day care is another, which is located away from the work-site but located conveniently to workers' residential areas or along transportation routes. The consortium model is a day care programme sponsored by several firms which combine to form a consortium and located off-site to all firms. The centre could be housed on-site at one firm.

Kindergartens

They are publicly or privately operated programme for four and five-year-old children prior to entrance into the primary school. The kindergartens are to provide a planned sequence of activities centred on talents (i.e. small blocks for building, developing mathematical concepts, and making designs), reinforced by occupation (i.e. craft work) as well as other activities, and surrounded by a verbal envelope (i.e. poems, songs, story telling and discussions).

Nursery School
Nursery school is the term applied to facilities planned for three and four-year-old children. Two-year-old children could be enrolled too in some cases.

Primary Schools
Although primary schools have continued to change with the demands of time, they are still the level at which skill subjects of reading, writing and arithmetic must be mastered and content subjects e.g. science and social studies, is introduced in a more structured atmosphere than is found in most pre-primary programmes.

The right of the Nigerian child to be educated from early childhood as an opportunity to train and mould the child for his or her future role as adult has almost been obliterated. Instead of engaging the children in early childhood education programmes, parents have resorted to abusing and neglecting them, this has left the children in despair and frustrating condition grasping for survival.

This has affected the physical, mental and social development of children — a trend, which is found to pose a threat to the social, economical and political fibre of the nation.

Learning and Development
Learning and child development is a process that requires the teachers' understanding as well as parents', and the society in general. It is one that demands patience, endurance and consistent follow-up to bring the best out of the child. For this reason, it is necessary that teachers and parents avail themselves the opportunity to learn and understand the needs and various developmental stages of the child.

More importantly, persons planning to become professional teachers in various educational levels should study foundation courses in psychology, philosophy, sociology and psychiatry, because these are the basis for understanding how children acquire knowledge, and also for comprehending children's intellectual and social growth and development.

From learning theories and from the normative — descriptive data collected by researchers on children's development, teachers are able to gain insight into the general characteristics of growing children. With such valuable knowledge, teacher-child relationship becomes one of cordiality and understanding, thereby creating a conducive learning environment for the child.

Children's experiences in school are being very much influenced by what the teacher regards as learning. The teacher has the responsibility of creating a stimulating environment that makes learning successful, because through interaction with the environment children learn.

Most of the time we wonder about certain questions, why does one child want to learn while another does not? Why does one child remember the events of a story while another forgets? How can more children be stimulated and aided to want to learn, to learn well, and to remember what they learn?

The answers to these questions actually are determined to a good extent by what the teacher understands about the learning process of the child. The teacher, therefore, has to know exactly what to do, what activity suits the talent of each child as to enhance such skill — this is what the learning process entails.

The learning process of a child's development is gradual but continuous, as captured by Agnes Snyder in her poetic statement:

> You cannot hurry human growth,
> It is slow and quiet,
> Quiet and slow,
> As the growth of the tree.

Principles of Learning

When a child is born he knows absolutely nothing. All knowledge is gathered after birth. Some of what he learns will come incidentally, such as the knowledge that being warm is more pleasurable than being cold. Some will be learned consciously, for example, when he goes off to find out what is making the interesting noise outside. Both of these kinds of learning, unconscious or casual, are the kinds that the school should provide.

Casual learning results from the experience of our environment and needs no effort. It just happens. Some psychologists believe that explains all the so called innate tendencies of man and the natural talents of individuals. Certainly, these characteristics could not reveal themselves apart from our conscious appreciation of our environment, though, it is probably going too far to say that they are born of environment.

Deliberate learning, on the other hand, does not just happen. It is caused, or as psychologists say, it is motivated. Casual learning is like a piece of driftwood swept down by a river. It's experience result from the haphazard interplay of the river currents and the riverbed and its banks. Deliberate learning results, however, only when you direct your learning along definite, planned channels.

Some of the things you learn you forget very quickly. Others make a deep and unforgettable impression. The depth of learning depends upon the total effect of the experience upon you. Learning is directly pre-operational to the force of the experience that causes it. This leads to the definition of what learning is; it is any change in behaviour that is due to experience.

At birth, although, the child knows nothing, his tiny body is wonderfully prepared for learning. All the senses are working and can respond to the environment with a repertoire of reflex behaviours. All his learning will grow out of the reaction of this infant response mechanism to the forces of our environment.

If we were to deal with all the experience that life offers for our learning, we would need to be superhuman. Since we are not, we start from birth to select from the great mass of experiences around us those that we can deal with, gradually enlarging our capacity as we go. As each experience comes to have meaning for you, it opens up the way for new selections and deeper understanding. So your knowledge grows and your skill to handle that knowledge develops.

Prerequisites for Efficient Learning

The three most important factors, which contribute to speedy, and effective learning, are readiness, motivation and activity.

Readiness is necessary for all learning. This depends on physical and mental maturation of the child and also on the accumulation of experience as a foundation for the building of new learning. For instance, you cannot teach a child to talk until maturation has done its work, and you cannot teach a child to read until he has established a certain degree of language skills.

One of the tasks of a teacher will be to recognise readiness in the child. There is no simple guide; it is a matter of experience by carefully observing and studying the child. Readiness in the child is often shown by an eager response to the learning task with which he is presented. It is always accompanied by rapid progress once learning is begun.

Lack of readiness may be due to lack of maturation or insufficient preparation of the child in those foundations of learning upon which the new learning will be built. The result will be painfully slow progress or complete absence of progress.

Motivation is very important in learning because it provides the power to the inner drives. But all motives are not equally strong and so for efficient learning, we have to concentrate on the strongest.

Motives may be either externally imposed or self-imposed. For example, we may do something because we have been told to do it or because we are anxious to do it. One is externally imposed, the other self-imposed. But the externally imposed may become self-imposed if we obey someone because we want to please him or her. Duty is a self-imposed motive. Generally speaking, self-imposed motives are necessary for efficient learning and a moderate amount of anxiety is beneficial.

The strongest motives arise from the strongest emotions we feel. A single lesson may be sufficient to make us learn and remember the truth for a lifetime. Weak motives often fail to establish learning, but even if they do, the lessons are forgotten easily soon. The difference lies in the strong personal involvement filed by the child in one case, and the absence of it in the other. Teachers must, therefore, seek to make the children become personally involved in the lessons.

The motives that energise our learning may change as the process of learning goes on. Two children may play with identical toys but one throws away his toy as soon as his initial curiosity has worn off. The other grows more and more curious with his. Curiosity changes to interest and pleasure as the motivation of his play. Teachers need to notice when the motives which at first stimulated their children's learning begin to falter. It is then that they must supply new motives, or better still, encourage their children to supply new and more vigorous motives. This is a task which requires individual attention.

The skill of a teacher lies in his ability to use the aims of the children to motivate their learning and thus, utilise the full energy of the children towards worthwhile learning. Teachers need to recognise that motivation is closely linked with aims and goals of the children as well as the teachers even though it may differ.

Nothing is learned unless we are active in it. We learn by doing, and we do what we learn. This is the test of true learning as opposed to the cloak of learning that so many people wear to cover their ignorance. Activity is not only playing games, jumping about and lots of noise making. Thinking too is an activity.

A very young child, however, can experience fully only what he does himself. He does not have sufficient experience to be able to relive the experiences of others whom he hears of, reads about, or even whom he sees.

Older children, on the other hand, can be moved to tears by a sad story or become enraged by an account of cruelty. They feel just as though they personally were experiencing the actions described because, they have sufficient experience to be able to share the feelings of other people. The lesson for the teacher from this is that he or she must choose activities which are suited to the age and experience of the children.

The need for activity in learning never ceases. In conscious learning there is nothing as a passive learner. The more active the child is, the more quickly he will learn.

Another feature of the need for activity in learning is in the use of practice and repetition. A great deal of our effective learning depends upon repeated experiences. For instance, memorisation such as we use when we learn a poem by heart, depends on our repeating it over and over again. We learn attitudes by repeated experiences of the same kind as we learn habits and skills by repeated practice. The more often we do something, the more established it becomes, as a part of our total learned ability. This helps to emphasise the importance of activity, both in doing and repetitive aspects as an integral part of the learning process.

Learning Process

There are different ways in which learning happens. The following are the main areas:

1. *Conditioning*

The new born baby is fed and nursed by his mother. She is the one who satisfies all his early needs. Quickly, he comes to associate her with the satisfaction of these needs and even the sound of her voice may be enough to settle him when he cries. He is learning through association or conditioning.

Learning by association or conditioning is a useful method for learning attitudes and habits. It is good for children to learn school lessons and the teacher has it in his power to achieve this. It is through conditioning that we react to certain things in a specific way so that, for example, when we see a snake we automatically jump. These reactions have been built up by the repeated use of the same response to a particular stimulus. They build up in our minds a system of associations so that when we see or hear anything, the appropriate response automatically leads to action.

2. *Training*

Training has much in common with conditioning because it is used in developing attitude, habits and skills. But training children to become obedient, respectful, quick readers or almost anything the teachers want shares with conditioning two main qualities — a system of punishments and rewards, and must be repeated frequently to become effective. It is important for teachers to note that, punishments and rewards must be appropriate to the age and character of the child.

There is need for consistency of practice in both conditioning and training, for the children must always receive the same or similar treatment so that habits develop. Inconsistent treatment greatly weakens the effectiveness of the method. The more often a child performs as he has been trained to, the more likely he will continue to do so even when training has stopped.

Training is the only kind of learning which has considerable transfer value. Training in qualities such as neatness, carefulness, persistence and punctuality have a high degree of transfer value to many school and day-to-day practices. The aim of training is to achieve efficiency of performance; the best possible standard with the least possible effort.

3. *Trial and Error Learning*

Faced with a new problem to solve by ourselves, our learning will nearly always be of this kind. The result of trial and error is an experience in which we tend to eliminate those activities that are unsuccessful and consolidate those that are successful. Trial and error is not an efficient method of learning, because it may take a long time before an individual hits on the best course of action.

However, the time and effort put into the unsuccessful attempts is not wasted because you must have enriched yourself with experiences of unknown things in the course of trying to be successful. Making mistake is part of learning. The element of discovery is of great psychological value as it thrills the individual. He has learned how to get it right and can enact this experience again with quick result.

To avert trial and error learning method, the teachers, in order to save time and make the activity less frustrating to some children, can give clues on how to arrive at the discovery. This is called guided discovery.

4. *Insight Learning*

This leads to a deeper understanding than is found with other forms of learning. Like trial and error learning, its outcome is a discovery. Insight comes when you can step back from your learning and look at your learning materials objectively. It usually comes as a flash of understanding as to what to do exactly to get to your goal. Insight is necessary for intelligent learning. It is like giving an exact clue to achieving an aim or goal.

The value of insight as a method of learning is its great speed and the depth of understanding that accompanies it. Understanding that may grow only slowly with other methods or, perhaps, never fully comes, arrives in a flash with insight. The teacher can assist greatly in encouraging this kind of learning among his children in all the subjects studied in school. The more he can help the child to recognise in his mind the new learning material with relevant knowledge he has gained in the past, the chance there is of him reaching the right conclusions and enjoying himself at the same time.

This depends entirely on the teacher's presentation of the learning materials. It, therefore, requires the teacher to carefully prepare the lessons, such that, the new lesson materials will be associated with knowledge gained in previous lessons. That is, the child should be able to use the knowledge gained from a previous lesson to come up with an insight on how to perform well in the activity before him. The teacher should clarify the relationships within the materials presented with a past activity.

5. Learning by Imitation

This is another quick way of learning though it does not share the depth of understanding that comes with insight. Opinions, belief and behaviour are often adopted quickly by people from others whom they admire.

There are good and bad ways for the teacher to encourage imitation amongst his children, for instance, he can present them with his own form of predigested knowledge and insinuate that it is "the whole truth and nothing but the truth".

This method of teaching weakens the critical faculty of the children, and takes away the desire to test and prove all things, which should be the mark of education. This leaves the children with a shallow understanding, which allows forgetting to get rid of the knowledge almost as quickly as it is learned.

On the other hand, the teacher can be a living example of the truths he tries to teach. The more practical form of learning by imitation comes in the use of demonstration. Showing how something is done is a much more effective way of teaching than describing how it is done. Demonstration may bring more trouble but it is quicker in the end.

6. Memorisation

Memorisation is a special kind of remembering. It is what is usually called "committing to memory" or "remembering by heart". Most children can memorise long texts and poems. The value of this, however, depends on the understanding that accompanies it. Without understanding, memorisation becomes merely vain babbling. Unfortunately, much of what passes for learning in schools is of this kind of memorisation without understanding.

There are principles, which if followed, make memorisation easier. They are:

a. Learning as Whole

If the child sees what he is trying to memorise as a meaningful whole, the task of learning is made easier. It must not be seen as parts of the whole.

b.   *Pattern Learning*
Pattern means any arrangement that is orderly. If the material that is to be memorised is arranged in some orderly way that gives it form or makes easy understanding, it is easier to remember. Any disorder makes it almost impossible to memorise.

But the most important point is that memorisation should be used for the right purpose. It is right for learning facts. But when it is used as an alternative to understanding how things are caused or why they happen, it is wholly wrong.

Learning Theories

What is a theory? A theory could be said to be an organised system of knowledge related to principles, or assumptions that is designed to explain how something works. In education, a theory is an idea, plan or scheme developed to explain how children learn, how they should be taught, and/or what they should be taught.

Let us then examine some of the learning theories of education, which can aid teachers and even parents in understanding what this learning process is all about. They will help in shaping our attitudes in response to the educational needs of the child to develop.

These learning theories (sometimes called systems) were developed from some philosophical views and were categorised as, (a) open theory, which states that the internal process in a human is what determines learning; (b) closed theory, which emphasises external forces that determine learning; and (c) transitional theory, which uses aspects of both open and closed theories.

Table 3.1: Influences upon Educational Thinking

OPEN SYSTEM	TRANSITIONAL SYSTEM	CLOSED SYSTEM
Phenomenology Child-centred	Progressivism Interactions Transactional Psychology	Behaviourism Cultural Transmission Mechanism Society-centred
Subjective psychology Rationalism Humans mould	Humanistic psychology Transcendentalism Humans mould	Objective psychology Analytic philosophy

environment	the environment Humans are moulded by the environment	Humans are moulded by the environment
Emphasis on internal states		Emphasis on internal states

Table 3.1 lists the concepts and people who have influenced learning theories from a philosophical and psychological viewpoint and categorise them by the type of learning system they represent.

The theories:

1. Acquisition of Knowledge and Skills (Mechanism)

Learning was seen as the same as knowing for many years past. This theory is based on the mental ability of the child to memorise and repeat to the teacher all what had been taught to the child. This is, even today, traditionally practised by most school children and it has influenced their learning processes. In a classroom set-up, children are required to recite certain lessons and even to memorise their textbook or information given them orally by their teacher.

The children's interests are not developed and they are not exposed to ways of solving problem on their own; a self-solving problems activities. Motivation is based upon regards and punishment; evaluation of learning is by formal tests of memory and class promotion usually result from the achievement of minimal marks. This is a closed system of learning.

2. Interactionism

It has been accepted in recent years that learning involves the moulding of behaviour also, which comes about through interaction with the environment. According to this theory, the acquisition of knowledge and skills represent only a part of the learning process. Learning is believed to take place only when an individual has an experience that influences behaviour and makes him or her a different person.

This system considers the influence of more factors in the learning environment than does the "learning is knowledge" concept. While it is true that a child may learn from a textbook, a child can as well learn from another child, from something seen, heard, touched or tasted outside the classroom.

Learning is a function of the child's total environment, as such, the learning experience has an effect on the character or personality of the child. If a child has really learned, he or she will behave differently in the future. This is an example of transitional theory.

3. **Rationalism**

The rationalistic concept emphasises that individuals mould their environment through thinking process — rational thinking. Learning takes place when teachers of other persons pose situations that require children to rationalise (think through) what is to be done. This is an open system.

4. **Behaviourism**

This concept is based on common assumption, be it called stimulus-response, conditioning, trial-and-error or bond psychology. It assumes that "wholes" are built from parts, and that learning is a process of adding up of experiences. The learner reacts as a collection of parts rather than as a unified "whole" (spirit, mind and body); repetition and drill precede learning. This is to say, the learner reacts in part in a given situation or experience. This is another of a closed system.

5. **Humanistic Psychology**

According to this view point, learning is a growth process and it is the outcome of inheritance, insight, maturation, and differentiation, rather than repetition. In the mental growth of the child, whole (spirit, mind and body) concepts come first; parts have meaning because of their relationship to the whole. For instance, the child's first concepts are class concepts, any animal may be called "dog". Later the concepts become specific and the child differentiates between "dog" and "cat".

Social studies unite experiences, learning to read through experience charts, and the teaching of whole concepts in maths, music, art, and language first, are all examples.

General Principles and Theories of Development

In order to understand human development, it is important to consider information on physical, biological, intellectual, social, emotional and other types of behavioural changes. These changes are the product of genetic factors, biological conditions, past experiences, present experiences, as well as the culture.

Developmental theorists have been influenced by some of these factors. The theorists to be discussed in this chapter are Erik H. Erikson and Jean Piaget. After explaining each of the theories, you will find a brief discussion of its educational implications.

Erikson's States of Psychosocial Development

Eriskson sees personal actualisation taking place only after an acceptable resolution of certain crises or basic psychological problems. A crisis is a time of increased vulnerability to a particular psychosocial problem. Each crisis is related to the others; each exists in some form before the decisive moment for its resolution arrives; and each, as it is positively resolved, contributes to the ultimate strength and vigour of the growing personality (Erikson, 1963).

Stages of Psychosocial Development

The following are some of the essential characteristics of the stages of personality development proposed by Erikson (1963):

Trust v. Mistrust (birth to 1 year)

Here, the quality of life, including love, attention, touch and feeding relationships, influence the child's fundamental and primitive feeling of trust or mistrust of the environment. These feelings are spread later in life. A favourable ratio of trust to mistrust is a form of psychosocial strength. For example, if the needs of infants are met and if the parents communicate genuine affection, children will think of their world as safe and dependable. On the other hand, if care is inadequate, inconsistent or negative, the children will approach their world with fear and suspicion.

Autonomy v. Shame and doubt (2 to 3 years)

At this stage, the child tests his parents and his environment, learning what he can control and what he cannot. Developing a sense of self-control without loss of self-esteem is necessary to one's feeling of free will. Excessive control by parents gives the child lasting feelings of doubt about his capabilities and shame about his needs or body. The child's feeling of autonomy grows out of his initial emancipation from his mother. It depends on the earlier development of trust rather than mistrust.

Initiative v. Guilt (4 to 5 years)

With a sense of trust and a feeling of autonomy, the child can develop a sense of initiative. He can go on his own into strange places and let curiosity run its course. A realistic sense of purpose emerges along with rudimentary forms of ambition. The development of initiative and the experience of guilt begin to form the conscience. The parents deny the child permission to do certain things as part of their response to his unbridled exploratory tendencies.

Thus, he learns the meaning of "No!" As he transgresses those prohibitions, in reality or fantasy, he feels guilt. The parent or teacher who blocks initiative too often may raise a guilt, rather than constricted child. On the other hand, the parent or teacher who rebukes too rarely may raise a child without a fully developed conscience. The outcome of a balanced resolution of the initiative versus guilt crisis is to:

> Free the child's initiative and sense of purpose for adult tasks which promise (but cannot guarantee) as fulfilment of one's range of capacities. This is prepared in the firmly established, steadily growing conviction undaunted by guilt, that "I am what I can imagine I will be" (Erikson, 1968, p. 122).

Accomplishment v. Inferiority (6 to 11 years)

The child must be able to do and make some things well, or even perfectly. Being kept from having feelings of accomplishment will lead to feelings of inferiority and inadequacy. Teachers in these years have the responsibility of creating successful experiences for each child, of keeping feelings of ineptness from forming. This requires knowing each student's capabilities as well as controlling the student's working environment. One particular danger noted by Erikson, is that work accomplishment will become an end in itself, stifling the person's further growth. Feelings of worth based only on work must be avoided.

Identity v. Confusion (12 to 18 years)

As young adults approach independence from parents and achieve maturity, they are concerned about what kind of person they are becoming. The growing and developing youths, faced with a physiological revolution within them, and with tangible and adult tasks ahead of them are now primarily concerned with what they appear to be, in the eyes of others and compared with what they feel they are. In their search for a new sense of continuity and sameness, adolescents have to re-fight many of the battles of earlier years. The goal is development of ego identity. The danger of this stage is role confusion, particularly, doubts about sexual and occupational identity. If adolescents succeed (as reflected by the reactions of others) in integrating roles in different situations to the point of experiencing continuity in their perception of self, identity develops. If they are unable to establish a sense of stability in various aspects of their lives, role confusion results. Failure to resolve this crisis prolongs adolescence and makes for inadequately functioning individuals who take on adult role without an integrated personality. These individuals will not cope effectively with the post-identity crises of the life cycle.

Intimacy v. Isolation (Young Adulthood)

The young adult emerging from the search for, and insistence on identity, is eager and willing to fuse his identity with others. Can one share by giving some piece of his own identity over to another, so that "we" supplants "I" in thinking about the present and future? Inability to develop intimate relationships leads to psychological isolation, which is less desirable, perhaps less healthy for the individual.

Generativity v. Stagnation (Middle Age)

Generativity refers to creativity, productivity, and an interest in guiding the development of the next generation. Maturity requires a dependent, one for whom you are mature. It also requires caring for and nurturing what is in your environment; ideas, things, and people. Without a preponderance of generative responses, the adult suffers boredom, apathy, pseudo-intimacy, interpersonal impoverishment, and a pervading sense of stagnation.

Integrity v. Despair (Old Age)

The personality is fully integrated when one develops a sense of acceptance of this one and only chance at life on earth, and of the important people in it. People and events must be taken at face value. One's children, spouse, parents, and job are what they are. Most importantly, in recognising this, one can say, "I am what I am!" In other words, responsibility for what you are is your own. At this stage you can have dignity. On the other hand, the development of desire, of unhappiness with yourself and with what you have wrought, can lead to a troubled, self-contemptuous, desperate end to the life cycle.

Generally, this theory of development includes all the possibilities of personality formation that are seen in people. Characteristics like trusting, stingy, creative, altruistic, complacent, wily, assertive, precarious, etc., can be seen to have roots in the various crises and resolutions described by Erikson.

Educational Implications of Erikson's Theory

Younger pupils should be provided plenty of opportunities so that they would develop a sense of independence. Reduce to the barest minimum any feelings of doubt or shame in the pupils. Even when a pupil gives a very wrong answer to a question, avoid altering statements that would make the pupil feel ashamed.

With older pupils, provide avenues for feelings of initiative and accomplishment to emerge. In addition, provide avenues for self-directed and self-selected activities. Give children sufficient time to complete a task on their own. Encourage feelings of initiative and accomplishment on the part of the children. Avoid giving them unnecessary restrictions and regulations.

Reduce, or better still, eliminate any feelings of inferiority on the part of children who do not do as well as others. Learning situations should be arranged in such a way that children compete with one another.

At all times, show personal interest in individual pupil. This will make them feel that they are recognised. Never ignore any of the pupils. Endeavour to address the students by name and comment favourably on their class work at all times.

Do all you can in the courses that you teach to expose students to various occupational choices available to them. Help students to gradually be prepared to continue their studies in post-secondary institutions.

Piaget's Stages of Cognitive Development

Jean Piaget (1890 - 1990), a Swiss psychologist, in his famous theory of how children learn and grow intellectually simply puts it that children, moving through stages of mental development, have different abilities at different stages.

Intellectual development occurs, according to target, because of two inborn attributes, which are called **organisation** and **adaptation**. Organisation is the building of simpler processes such as seeing, touching, naming, and hearing, into higher-order mental structures. Through these processes, an individual composes his or her own system of understanding the environment. Adaptation is the continuing change that occurs in an individual as a result of interactions with the environment. Adaptation occurs as the individual:

a. Assimilates experiences;
b. Fits them into existing mental structures; and
c. Modifies the mental structures that do not fit so that they are ready for inclusion of the experience.

Mental development is influenced by four interrelated factors; maturation, experience, social interaction and equilibration, which is the joining of the previous three factors to build and rebuild mental structures.

Piaget's Stages

Piaget observed that intellectual development has four major stages: sensori-motor, pre-operational, concrete operational, and formal operational. Each stage has age designations, which are approximate. In addition, a stage does not end suddenly. It rather tails off. This means that a child could still be pre-operational in his thinking in certain areas while performing more logically in others.

First Stage

Sensori-motor

This stage covers approximately from birth to two years. It is characterised by the child's growth in ability in simple perceptual and motor activities. This is characterised by the development of schemes primarily through sense and motor activities. Children move from a newborn reflex activity to a more highly organised kind of activity. The child learns to:

- See himself as different from the object that is around him
- Seek stimulation by lights and sounds
- Try to prolong interesting experiences
- Define things by manipulating them, and
- Regard an object as constant, despite changes in its location or the

child's point of view.

Knowledge for the child under two years of age consists of the repertoire of actions upon objects in the environment. What a child does, from his simplest grasping through his non-complex examinations of things, is designed to give him mastery over his environment. Examining small changes in behaviour gives us indications as to what a child is learning and how that learning fits within more complex learning.

Second Stage
Pre-operational

This second stage covers the ages from two to seven years. In this stage, the child gradually acquires the ability to conserve and decentralise, but is not yet capable of operations (reversibility).

The principle of conservation refers to the idea that mass or substance does not change when the shape or appearance of the object is transformed. To illustrate this principle of conservation, pour water in two containers. The first container is a tall and narrow jar while the second is a short but bulky tube. Children at this stage would say that the tall narrow jar contains more water. This is because they concentrate on one quality; height.

Decentralisation is the ability to centre attention on more than one quality. As children in this state grow older, they are able to take into account both volume and height. They are able to understand that the amount of water remains, the same even though the shape of the water is changed.

Third Stage
Concrete Operational

Children at this stage are between seven and eleven years. Piaget uses the concept of operation in explaining how conservation is mastered. One major characteristic of an operation is its reversibility. Reversibility deals with awareness that conditions can be mentally reversed. In other words, the child can remember what conditions were like before they were reversed or changed. Thus, an operation is a mental action that can be reserved. It is a manipulation of objects or their internal representations. The child is capable of various logical operations but only with concrete things, although, the child can handle classification and grasp the principles involved. In other words, the child has problems with highly abstract thought.

Fourth Stage
Formal Operational
This stage covers the ages from eleven to fourteen. This is the final stage of cognitive development which Piaget calls "formal thought". Here, the student becomes increasingly capable of dealing with abstractions and formulating, and testing hypotheses. Formal thought is characterised by all systematic approach to problem solving, consideration of several variables at a time, as well as the ability to generalise by applying principles to many different situations.

Learning in the Pre-operational Stage
This is a stage of initiative thought, which happens to be a time when intellectual growth of children occurs (ages of two to seven). It is during this period that certain qualities have to be watched out for, in order to understand the progression of the child. Specific qualities such as classification and relationships, language, honesty, numbers, thinking and reasoning, acceptance and obedience, rules and games, social behaviour, guilt and punishment, and competition.

Examining them in relation to this stage is necessary for proper understanding.

Classification and Relationship Skills
There is a rapid development of this at this stage and the children can now make collections of information within which they can group and re-group for learning. Most children of two to five years old can not arrange things orderly, but at six years they can accurately place things in one to one relationship, though on trial and error basis.

Language
There are two types of verbal language-communicative speeches, which transmit information or ask questions. Egocentric speech is a monologue or mimicking of sounds and words, which accounts for about 40% of

children's speech at this pre-operational stage. The children talk to themselves most of the time. Children within this age range of two to seven years do not have the ability to listen accurately and find it difficult to understand or remember direction randomly. They act one step at a time. At this stage too, they use verbal mental images and more sophisticated words and expressions, which they may not understand. Arguments are normal, and can cause bad feeling.

Honesty
This, including knowledge of the difference between fact and fiction, is not a common trait of children within two to seven years. It is not that these children want to lie or deceive somebody, but they just get facts mixed up.

Educational Implications of Piaget's Theory
Educators have used Piaget's theory of cognitive development to develop a variety of curriculum materials at appropriate levels of difficulty for children at different educational levels. Piaget concluded that children should be given the opportunity to organise and adapt experiences in their own way. The open education movement is based on this fundamental assumption. In open education, children are allowed to choose most of their learning experiences. This is why they arrange activity centres in different parts of the classroom. Children at a particular level of cognitive development are encouraged to teach some things to one another.

Pre-school, kindergarten as well as most children in primary one and two are at the pre-operational level. They are capable of using symbols to stand for objects which make mental manipulation possible.

The type of thinking of each child in the class should be assessed. Learning through activity and direct experience is very essential. The children should be provided plenty of assorted materials and opportunities to learn on their own. Social interaction should be their own. Social interaction should be encouraged so that the children can learn from one another.

Secondary school students are mostly at the formal operational state. They are able to deal with obstructions, form hypotheses and consider possibilities. Students should be asked to explain how they arrived at solutions to problems. Students should be taught how to be more systematic about solving problems. The step-by-step procedure of solving problems should be emphasised.

Numbers
Most teachers of young children believe that once a child begins counting numbers, they can learn basic number facts. But this is surprisingly not so, because counting and conservation of number do not follow each other. Though, regular classroom teachers have it that children of age six years can add and subtract, the problem is their being able to conserve, that is to realise that the numbers do not change when the objects are rearranged.

Thinking and Reasoning
Children at this stage lack logical thinking and reasoning in doing things and this worries the adults.

Acceptance and Obedience
These are slow to develop and sometimes non-existent in children age two and three. Children of aged four and five see acceptance and obedience as normal reactions to adult authority. By ages six and seven, this total acceptance of adult authority begins to weaken, although generally children in this age group obey adults.

Rules and Games
As the child becomes more social, it becomes necessary that rules and games are learned. Children at this stage will break the rules of a game because they cannot remember two things at once; what they want to do and how to do it.

Social Behaviour
This changes at ages six and seven from self-centred play to more participatory ones. At this pre-operational stage, the children are highly imitative, a weird noise, a funny face, or a funny walk will cause laughing and imitation of the noise or gesture.

Guilt and Punishment
These are normal to children's minds. In their minds, guilt is being caught misbehaving, and misbehaving is just disobeying adult rules. Therefore,

punishment is natural, expected, and necessary.

Competition
These children don't go into competition in either work or play because they mean nothing to them. They play or work for the fun of it.

Development and Growth
To be able to assess or review the development and growth performance of a child, it is necessary to maintain a descriptive data that contains the characteristics of the children — physical, emotional, intellectual, and interpersonal. It is from this information that the teacher is able to prescribe the programme, activities, methods, and materials to be used in the classroom. Such data is called Normative - descriptive data. This is a research data on development and growth of children.

Normative - Descriptive Data
Despite the fact that individual children may not fit these general normative patterns exactly, it is still useful for the teacher to know the general characteristics of young children of the same age. By using this research data to compare with classroom observations, the teacher can now know some severe deficiencies in a particular child. This insight will also help the teacher in coming up with programmes, activities, and methods that will suit the need of each child in the classroom.

The following descriptive research data may be used by the teacher as a research standard, to compare with classroom observations, to gain insight into the characteristics of the children he or she teaches. This insight will aid established goals.

Three-Year-Old Children

Physical
This age of children maintain a better balance and equilibrium than two years old when running, after they have gained greater body activity and improved co-ordination. They are more vigorous and boisterous and like to play with large blocks, wagons, slides and other equipment that can develop their large muscles. They are more skilful with their hands and can draw crude pictures with crayons. They enjoy using clay to create.

Emotional

A two-year-old child, like saying "no", but at three, children like to give and share. They are more co-operative and conform, though they still have difficulty handling their emotion. They have anger, which seldom happen and do not last long. They can be jealous of a young brother or sister. Because they are curious, they can become unintentionally destructive.

Intellectual

They understand simple questions, statements and directions. They ask many questions and understand more words than they use. Abstract words are beyond their understanding.

Interpersonal

They have a great desire to please, mother is their best companion and they look to her for security, recognition, and encouragement. Three-year-old children like parallel play but are beginning to share and take turns.

Four-Year -Old Children

Physical

This age of children becomes more noisy, speedy and stormy as the days pass. They hit, kick, jump up and down, and love to dash off in the opposite direction. Throwing stones or breaking something is fully intentional destructive action this time. They are equally becoming skilful in body movements such as skipping, running, or jumping, all at risky speed. They like to throw balls, cut, saw, lace, colour, and build with small blocks.

Emotional

These children are not too concerned about the feelings of others and are not very sensitive to praise or blame. Sometimes they praise themselves by bragging. They like to pursue their own course, and occasional frustrations don't bother them much.

Intellectual

They constantly ask questions. They have limitless imagination and tell a mixture of truth and fiction. With their imaginary friends, they have fun.

They do not like repetition, and so go from one activity to the other. Dramatising simple stories, group singing about everyday experiences, and informational material delights them.

Interpersonal
They are defiant ("No, I won't!"), but they still want to be like others in the group. They like taking trips and can call people silly names or become very bossy and naughty.

Five-Year-Old Children

Physical
They are poised and controlled and can swing, climb, jump, and skip with dexterity. Purposeful activities are busily engaged in, such as drawing, colouring, painting, cutting, and pasting, which are all great fun to these children. Activities like riding, pushing wheeled toy, copying of designs, letter, numbers, puzzle, and printing their names are delightful to them. They are able to dress, wash, and feed themselves. They use tools too.

Emotional
These are more conservative in their actions than the four year old children and they are interested in home activities, therefore like to help. They love babies and play a lot with dolls.

Intellectual
These children are still factual and literal and do not ask many questions. They enjoy stories that are short, real and possible, full of action, and are in the present. They may be slow in action, but are persistent because they usually have an idea of what they are going to do.

Interpersonal
They are often friendly, but shy with strangers. They like best to play with their age mates. They want to be good but can't always differentiate right from wrong, such that, when something goes wrong, they may blame the nearest person.

Six-Year-Old Children

Physical
There is marked physical growth at this age. Large muscles are better developed than small muscles, but eye-hand co-ordination is not well established. They wiggle and squirm and may have awkward and clumsy behaviour.

Emotional
Their feeling patterns go from one extreme to another, from smiles to tears, from love to hate, and they express these with vigour. Emotionally, they are still attached to home and are full of inconsistencies; they want to be big and small, at the same time they want to be independent and yet dependent. They can't make decisions as easily as when at age five. They are usually eager and enthusiastic about new things or actions.

Intellectual
Their favourite question is "Why?" They try to answer by themselves questions they asked without seeking help. Their listening vocabulary is large and concrete, but their use of the vocabulary is limited. They are able now to make connection between spoken and printed words. They have little idea of time and space and have wide range of interest. They like using crayons and pencils and prefer real stories to be told over and over again.

Interpersonal
They are becoming mindful of social approval and many join in forming gang. Fighting to attract attention is common place and they tease a lot. They seldom want to give up their place. Their best friends are usually the same sex/gender with them.

REFERENCES

Adams, J.F 1973. *Understanding Adolescence.* Boston: Allyn and Bacon.

Atkinson, J.W. 1964. *An Introduction to Motivation.* Princeton, N.J.: Van Nostrand.

Badmus, A. and Odediran, N.O. 2000. *A General Introduction to the Theory and Practice of Education.* Ilorin: Ahnour International.

Bigge, M.L. 1971. *Learning Theories for Teachers.* New York: Harper & Row.

Charles, C.M. 1976. *Individualizing Instruction.* St Louis: C.V. Mosby.

Coles, R. 1970. *Erik H. Erikson: The Growth of His Work.* Boston: Little, Brown.

Dubey, D.L., Dubey, O.E.C. and Ndagi, J.O. 1985. *Teaching in the Primary School: A Course for Active Learning.* London: Longman Group Ltd.

Erikson, E. 1968. *Identity: Youth and Crisis.* New York: Norton.

Erikson, E. 1963. *Childhood and Society.* New York: Norton.

Holt, J. 1967. *How Children Learn.* New York: Pitman.

Jersild, A. 1968. *Child Psychology.* 6th ed. Englewood Cliffs, N.J.: Prentice Hall.

Maslow, A.H. 1954. *Motivation and Personality.* New York: Harper.

Okoh, N. 1983. (ed). *Professional Education: A Book of Readings.* Benin City: Ethiope Publishing Co.

Chapter Four

STAGES OF CHILD DEVELOPMENT

Physical Development

Stages in Physical Development
The physical development of the child begins at conception. From that moment he or she begins to increase in size and weight and complexity until he is fully grown about the age of twenty. During this period, the child's body does not grow uniformly. Some parts mature before others and so, at no state does the child have a body of reduced adult proportions. A child of two or three years enlarged geometrically to adult size would look grotesque.

On the other hand, some parts of a child's body are fully grown at birth and do not change during his or her life. The inner ear structure of the newborn baby is an example of this for it is identical in size with that of the adult. Strange still, some organs are present in the young child, which later disappear in the adult. The thymus gland, for example is present in the infant, but when this persists into adulthood, it becomes a fatal danger to the individual in cases of shock.

The physical development of the child, if it proceeds normally, may be thought of as moving from one rung to the next of a ladder. As each stage is reached, it brings the next within reach, so that progress is continued from elementary reflexes of the new born baby, through the sitting, standing, walking, and running stages, and so to the complex feats of the athlete and juggler.

The main stages in the physical development of the child are summarised below in table 4.1.

Table 4.1: **Stages in Human Physical Development**

	AGE	PHYSICAL CHARACTERS	ACHIEVEMENTS
PRE-NATAL	-3 months	Union of male sperm with female ovum (less than the size of the head of a pin)	Conception
	-6 months	Large head with eyes, nose and mouth evident. Whole body about 76.2 mm long. Weight about 28.35kg	Heart beating
	-9 months	Limbs developed hands and toes evident. Body about 0.53m long. Weight about 1.36kg	Movements of body and limbs discernible
BIRTH		Possesses all the physical characteristics of humans but out of proportion compared with adults. Height about 0.46m weight about 2.95kg	Survives the physical strains of birth. Breathes air, feed by mouth, cries, sees, hears, feels, tastes and can smell.
	+3 months	Increases in height to about 0.53m and in weight to 4.99kg	Can kick legs vigorously, roll over form lying on back, lift head and smile.
	+6 months	About double birth weight. First teeth may appear	Can sit by itself. Can be weaned gradually.
	+9 months	Rate of physical growth begins to slow down	Can stand with help. Crawls
	1 year	Rate of physical growth further reduced	Stands by himself and may even walk alone.
	2 years	Steady increase in size	Learns to run

CHILDHOOD	2-5 years	Continued steady increase in size	Improves in running. Learning to jump and throw
	6-12 years	Rate of physical growth slows down but consolidation continues	Co-ordination develops further, making skills like reading and writing possible.
ADOLES-CENCE	12-16 years	Sex organs develop. Hair begins to grow on various parts of the body as on adults.	Muscular co-ordination improves
		Body proportions begin to approach those of the adult	
YOUTH	16-21 years	Height growth ceases but consolidation increase weight slightly	All skills within the range of the individuals. Training in skills like games and athletics can result in rapid improvement and the achievement of high standards

1. *Pre-natal (From Conception to Birth)*

During this period, the child grows from a single tiny cell to a baby. Although his or her sex is determined at conception, this can be seen in the foetus only about three months before birth. During the last three months before birth, the child will double its weight, increase in size about fifty per cent and be prepared for the great day of birth.

The lung will be made ready for breathing air, the digestive system for feeding from his or her mouth instead of through the umbilical cord and the bones will gradually harden. Even if born two months earlier than the expected date, a baby can survive if given special attention and care.

2. *Infancy (Birth to 2 Years)*
The child at birth seems small and helpless but all the senses function and the body is capable of considerable activities, including reflex actions like crying, grasping, blinking and those associated with feeding. During this period, the child triples his or her birth weight and learns to respond much more specifically to the messages received by the senses than he or she did at birth. He or she will end up being fully weaned and being able to live on a ratio of sleep to activity of about 3:2 as compared with 40:1 at birth.

3. *Childhood (2-12 Years)*
As the child grows older, his or her rate of increase in size and weight is slowed down. But in fact, at the age of three, the child would have reached about half his or her adult height.

The period of childhood is often divided into two periods, from two to five years and from six to twelve years, called early-childhood and later-childhood respectively. The changes in the early period are more dramatic. In it, the child gains control or a semblance of it, over his or her body so that he or she learns to run, jump, throw, and to control the eyes so that he or she can concentrate them on small objects. But in the latter, he improves his control so that he becomes better skilled in these activities. His or her muscles grow in strength so that he or she can do more and do better.

4. *Adolescence (12-16 Years)*
The physical changes, which herald sexual maturity, are the most important at this period. But the child's body continues to grow in size until it approaches full adult size. The boy parts company with the girls in physical development. The latter's performance in physical activities like racing, jumping and throwing may not improve, whereas the boy's does and his interest in sports and games may become excessive and people describe him as " 'mad' or 'keen' " on football.

5. *Youth (16-21 Years)*
The period brings to an end the physical growth of the individual, apart from the increase in weight that accompanies sedentary habits or

excessive food intake. It is a quiet period externally, but within, there is a maturing of the body and an improvement in co-ordination, which make possible high standards of athletic performance in both boys and girls.

Heredity and Physical Development

You may have sometimes wondered why you were born a human-being and not a goat or a fish. You may also have wondered why people do not remain as babies but grow up into adults, or why some people are handsome and others are ugly. The answer to all these questions in physical terms, is heredity.

You developed as a human being because you were conceived by the fertilisation of your human mother's ovum by your human father's sperm; the only creature that can develop when these unite is a human baby. Only human sperm can fertilise human ovum, just as only the sperm of goats can fertilise the ovum of goats. There can be no crossing of species. You have grown up because of your body's built-in mechanism of growth patterned on that of your ancestors.

Hidden in these reproductive cells are many of the characteristic features of the person from whom they come and these in turn are like those of his or her parents and so on, back in decreasing digression to his or her ancient forefathers. This heredity can be traced to two tiny parts of the muscles of the ovum and sperm cells known as chromosomes and genes. These two determined all our physical characteristics.

Genes are contained in the chromosomes and they cause some cells to develop into muscles, others to brain, bone, nerves, skin, etc. They therefore affect our shape and size, our mental ability and even our potential talents. If the genes do not act properly they produce serious abnormalities. It will be seen that from conception, we receive all our physical characteristics as a result of heredity.

At birth, a child has certain reflex actions such as the grasping slightly of anything placed in his or her hand, the sucking of any object put into his or her mouth or the contraction of the pupils of the eye in response to light. These reflexes are not learned but are inherited and are common to all human beings. Many of our inherited characteristics are not evident at birth.

Abnormalities may be handed down from parents to children. Idiocy, limb deformity, colour blindness, weak hearts and so forth sometimes run in families. When this is so, it is almost certain that the cause is heredity.

Environment and Physical Development

Environment influences our development throughout our whole life, because the fertilised cell responds to its environment throughout all the stages of its existence from conception to death. Before birth, it grows into the foetus or unborn child within the environment of the womb. This environment depends on the health of the mother and varies according to her diet and activities. Adverse conditions in the pre-natal environment may cause some abnormalities such as blindness, mental deficiency or physical damage.

After birth, the child is subjected to a much more complicated environment composed of physical, emotional and social forces. The physical environment experienced varies greatly from one person to another even in the same family. What we eat and how we live greatly affect our physical development.

In the effect of heredity and environment, choice has an influence which is less in the case of heredity than with environment. Man, of all creatures, is the most free to choose his environment and the most bale to adapt it into his wishes. Choice is a factor we must take into consideration in any study of environment effects.

Physical Maturation

As we grow older, it becomes possible for us to learn more and more skills. This time lag in achieving our ultimate capacity is due to what psychologists call "Maturation". By this, they mean the physical development of the muscles and the co-ordinating system for their control that take place in a growing child quite apart from physical exercise. As a result of maturation, activities become possible which hitherto were physically impossible. No amount of practice or encouragement will enable a six month old child to walk.

Examples of maturation are to be seen in the muscle development and co-ordination required to make walking and reading possible. Because these activities are dependent upon maturation, it is a mistake to try to hurry the child. You must wait until the child is ready at various stages of physical development. Readiness is usually indicated by the child's desire

Children who are launched into an activity, for which maturation has not prepared them, often end up by succeeding later than usual by developing attitudes which prevent learning. This underlines the importance of respecting the individuality of the child in teaching and awaiting the natural preparations the body makes for learning new skills.

Training in skills will only be rewarded when the necessary maturation has already taken place. That is why teaching children to read before they go to school is of little value. In fact, it often has an adverse effect. In the same way, the intensive training by which athletes improve their performance is of no use with children. To be of value, it must wait until the muscles have reached the state from which they benefit from intensive training, and that is not until after the age of sixteen. Once maturation has taken place, a person is capable of rapid learning and good performance so long as the training is appropriate.

Mental Development

Stages in Mental Development

Just as the physical development of the child can be traced through a number of stages, so his mental development follows similar patterns of periods, some of surging progress and others of quiet consolidation.

The power of the mind is rooted in the brain, but it is dependent upon the whole body for its expression. Your mind would be of little use to you if you could not hear or speak, or if you could not move even the smallest

The link between the brain and the body is the nervous system. The brain nerves reach out from the brain to every part of the body. Some are responsible for carrying to the brain every sensation of pain, sound, right, touch, taste and smell at speeds of up to 20 m.p.h. from the receptors or never endings found all over the surface of your body. Others, called effectors, carry the orders from your brain to muscles in your body so that you can wink, smile, cry, run or do what you please.

Almost everything you do, whether consciously or unconsciously, is the result of the activity of the mind channelled to the movable parts of your body through the nervous system. Because movement is involved, psychologists call this "motor activity" as opposed to the activity like thought, reasoning, remembering and so on, which can be isolated in the brain.

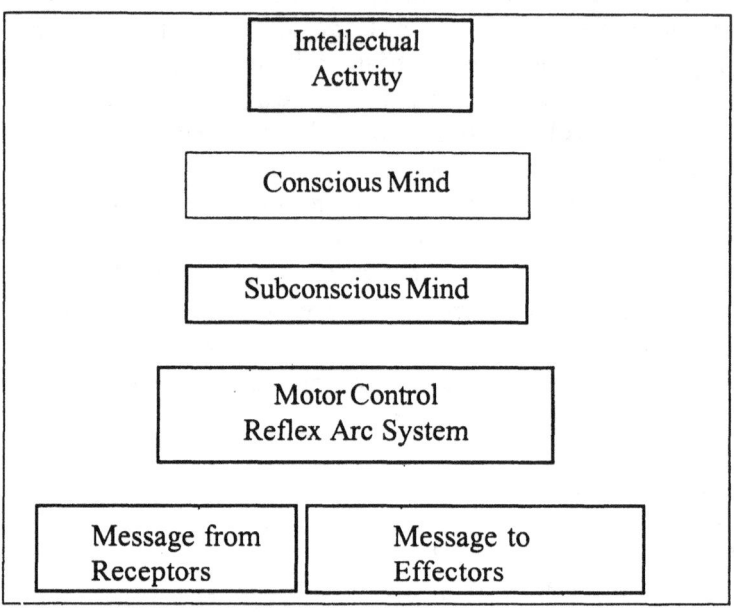

Fig. 4.1. The Relationship of Motor Activity

Fig 4. 1. Shows the relationships of motor activity, which involves the lower art of the central nervous system and intellectual activity, which can be linked with whole system, or isolated at will to the upper part.

Reflexes are the only motor actions or activities which short-circuit the brain. Instead, the message from the receptors passes directly to the effectors. It is through the independent intellectual activity of the brain, that you learn from experience and plan your future activities. Your mind can be a whirl of activity without a muscle of your body moving. It is this ability to think, rather than simply react physically that makes men much more adaptable.

It will be seen then, that in man and the child for that matter, the central nervous system has two main functions, namely; motor control and intellectual activity, the one concerned with responding, reacting, performing and the other concerned with thinking, understanding, planning and so forth. An understanding of these two functions is important in any study of children and the "why" they learn.

The central nervous system is an integral part of the body, so you should not think of mental development as something apart from physical development. However, for convenience, we can trace the mental development of the child through certain stages like those considered in relation to physical development. They are summarised in Table 4.2.

Table 4.2: Stages in Human Mental Development

	AGE	MENTAL CHARACTERISTIC	ACHIEVEMENTS
PRE-NATAL	-3 months -6 months	Growth of brain begins Nervous system exists in simplified form	Heart beating
	-9 months	Brain nearly completely formed	Reflex actions such as a grasping and withdrawal
BIRTH		Nervous system complete but brain weighs only approximately one-quarter of adult brain.	All reflex actions developed, such as breathing, crying, sucking, swallowing, digesting, elimination from bladder and bowels
			All sense organs respond to stimulation.
INFANCY	+3 months	Brain grows in size and weight and responds to environment	Generalised movements only. No proper control
		Continued growth and responsiveness	Learning more obvious
	+9 months	Growth continues	Improved control over motor activities, e.g. vocal organs begin to produce syllables
	+18 months	Growth continues	Vocabulary of over 200 words

CHILD-HOOD	2-years	Growth continues	Vocabulary of about 900 words. Vocabulary grows rapidly
	4-5 years	Increasing curiosity and thirst for knowledge	Speech is made in proper sentences
	6-12 years	Brain almost full-grown. Curiosity continues	Great increase in factual knowledge, beginning of reason
ADOLE-SCENCE	12-16 years	Growing mental independence	Sometimes a reversal of co-ordination with adverse effects of games and athletic skills particularly with girls. Further increase in knowledge and development of intellectual activities
YOUTH	16-21 years	Mature attitudes and behaviour develop	High degree of co-ordination, making possible high performance in skills. Further increase in knowledge and intellectual activities

1. *Pre-natal (From Conception to birth)*

The brain is the first mechanism of the body to develop following conception. Even as early as five months before birth when the child is only, little developed, he is capable of responding to a stimulus applied to his face. Gradually, the whole nervous system develops, so that even a month or so before birth, the child is capable of all the motor activities that are necessary for survival at birth.

2. Infancy (Birth to 2 Years)

At birth, although the child passes all the reflex activities that enable him to survive, his knowledge is absolutely nil. The result is that his behaviour at first is entirely reflex. He has no control over it.

During the first two years of life the child learns to sit, stand, crawl, walk and talk. What really happens is that his brain gains sufficient control over his growing body, limbs, and vocal organs to do these things. Motor control is the chief product of this stage. There is little visible evidence of intellectual activity.

3. Childhood (2 - 12 Years)

In this period the child launches out into an intensive search for knowledge. Questions like "Why?" and "What?" are constantly on his lips. "Lets find out", seems to be his philosophy of life.

As a result, his knowledge increases rapidly and his experience grows sufficiently to allow abstract thought.

The greatest mental achievement in early childhood is the conquest of language. This, together with the help of physical maturation, brings within reach of the child, the learning of other forms of language skills like reading and writing. As he passes from early childhood to later childhood, the beginning of abstract thought are made possible for the child by his growing control of language and concepts that are an integral part of abstract thought.

4. Adolescence (12-16 Years)

The rapid changes taking place in the child's body during this period are often reflected in an apparent out-of-step relationship between mind and body. The activity of the mind and its demands upon the body may over tax the physical changes taking place in the child's body and often make his muscular co-ordination seem awkward, but this is just a phase.

Adolescence, with its physical changes is often associated with emotional effects caused by the intensity with which the young child finds his feelings working in him. But it is a period whose beginning and end are difficult to determine precisely because adolescence merges imperceptibly into the neighbouring periods of childhood and youth.

However, during it, his growing experience makes him increasingly capable of abstract thinking.

5. *Youth (16 - 21 Years)*
The final stage in growing up is marked by the attainment of harmony between body and mind. Individuals are capable of high performance in physical skills. In creative work too, the individual may reveal evidence of latent talents. Intellectual activity becomes more vigorous, or potentially so, and youths feel more confident of their ability. All that is lacking is the depth and breadth of experience that makes men wide and fits the mature adult of posts of responsibility.

Heredity and Mental Development
The brains of men of high intelligence have been compared after death with those of the mentally defective and it has been found that the size of an individual's brain bears no direct relation to his mental ability.

The brain is the focal point of the whole nervous system. Our learning, thinking, remembering and behaviour all arise from the activity of the brain, and so, our ability and standard of performance in them depends upon the quality of the brain we are born with. This brings us right back to heredity.

There is evidence to show that our brains are the result of heredity in much the same way as our bodies. Just as some physical deformities run in families, so do some forms of mental defectives. The chances that intelligent parents will have intelligent children are the same as that tall parents will produce tall children. It is clear that mental development has strong links with heredity.

In any large number of unselected people, you will find that the distribution of intelligence follows the usual bell-shaped normal distribution curve, typical of other measurable physical qualities. Thus, by definition, near average intelligence includes the great majority of people; only relatively few will be found outside the range of normality, either being of very high or very low intelligence.

Heredity sets the potential limits of mental capacity. Whether these limits are reached or not depends on the environment. Genius is produced by the rare combination of chromosomes and genes to form a pattern of a particular kind. The chances of its happening to your child are similar to the possibility of our dealing with them; from half a pack of cards, all the aces and highest cards in the pack.

Environment and Mental Development

Just as the unborn child, during the months of pregnancy exists and develops physically in the environment of his mother's womb and is affected by her health, so the child's mental development is affected by his pre-natal environment. It sometimes happens that a mother contracts a disease and with this particular disease, there is danger that it may damage the brain of the child. Unfortunate physical and mental effects upon children have likewise been traced to drugs taken by mothers during pregnancy. These are environmental effects.

After birth, the child's environment is immensely broadened, and he is subjected to constantly changing physical, emotional and social experiences. These influence his mental development. It has been shown that conditions of diet, sleep, health and social contacts all have an influence upon his mental development. These forces of environment may be favourable or adverse accordingly, as they feed or starve his mind with these necessities for proper growth. Because at birth the child knows nothing, all his knowledge must be learned.

Consequently, behaviour, which is the individual's response to learning, develops relatively slowly and uncertainly at first. The task of learning from experiences is made easier if the same or similar experiences come frequently. It is accomplished sooner if these experiences produce an intense response, because then selecting the appropriate response becomes a matter of urgency.

Heredity determines the capacity for an individual's learning. Environment enables him to attain these limits or fall short of them as the case may be. Many genius died undiscovered because environment had never given them the opportunity to develop their talents. Choice plays a part in mental development. Within limit, the individual can choose the kind of environmental stimuli by which he learns, and the response which he makes to them. For example, a child chooses his playmates the way he spends his leisure, the book he reads, the job he does, and so on.

Mental Maturation

Although mental development is the product of learning, it nevertheless depends on the normal physical maturation of the brain and nervous system. Response to external stimuli is not possible until the receptors have grown sufficiently to do their job and the effectors have likewise developed. This primitive stage is reached before birth, but a great deal of refinement of the motor processes and those parts of the brain that deal with intellectual activities such as learning, thinking, and remembering must take place before the adult or mature state is reached.

When maturation has prepared the physical and mental links for a particular activity, training produces the skill with comparative ease. Without maturation no amount of training would succeed. Training simply determines how the child performs what he is potentially capable of. It is as though maturation opens all the gates along the paths of the nervous system used for particular activity.

An example of mental maturation is found in the readiness for speech found in children between the age of one and two. Before this stage is reached, the vocal organs are all complete; the links between them and the brain are also ready. What is lacking is the growth of associations in the mind between sounds and meaning. If deafness prevents the development of this association, he will be dumb even though his vocal organs may be quite normal.

But it has been shown by modern techniques in teaching the deaf and dumb, that the potential control by this kind of child over his vocal organs is ready just as the normal child. He can be taught to speak almost as soon and as well as the normal child, as long as the barrier of his deafness can be overcome. However, no child can learn to speak until a certain degree of maturation in the association parts of the brain has made this possible. Some mentally deficient people, because of this, never learn to speak properly and children of low intelligence speak poorly.

Reading, which is the ability to interpret meaning from visual symbols, is a progression from the interpretation of what is observed in reality to an understanding meaning, from symbols which of themselves bear no likeness to the original. This is not just a matter of training. Some children who are taught to read too early end up unable to read for meaning, although they can say the sounds. Sometimes, as a result of being forced into reading before they are ready, these children develop a lifelong aversion to reading.

For the teacher, the importance of all these lie in the realisation that a child may be too young to be taught. To try to teach such a child is

Stages of Child Development

wasted effort. Indeed, the reaction on the child's part to premature teaching may make successful teaching more difficult later on.

Physical and mental maturation of the normal child are closely linked, and it is unusual for one to proceed much more rapidly than the other. When this does happen, however, it is usually mental development that does not keep pace. This phenomenon produces people with adult physique but childish minds.

The maturation of the normal child is shown diagrammatically in Table 4.3

Table 4.3: Maturation of the Normal Child

1 and over	Ready for anything
16 – 21	Ready for abstract thinking
11 – 16	Ready for reasoning in concrete terms
6-11	Ready for skills requiring good co-ordination, such as reading and writing
3 – 6	Ready for memorization
1 – 2	Ready to relate meaning to words
Up to 1	Co-ordination begins the way for speech prepared

Intelligence

You probably have a good idea what you mean when you say that someone is intelligent, but you may find the greatest difficulty in trying to say what you mean by intelligence. Psychologists have had the same trouble and have had to resort to describing what it can do rather than saying what it is.

The definition of intelligence as the power to think is inadequate because it fails to recognise the finer activities of thinking, such as, comprehension, reasoning, the ability to grasp relationships, select relevant data, and fray generalisations from them.

And so psychologists have found themselves forced in their definitions of intelligence to include more and more, the things that man's intellect can do. The result is that intelligence is now regarded as, "a fluid collection of infinitely varied thinking abilities, and the measured intelligence of any individual depends on which thinking abilities are tested". This is Professor P. E. Vernon's conclusion.

More than fifty digits after only one look at some people, their general intelligence is often quite normal and they may not even be able to cook food for themselves. The same is found with some mathematical geniuses who can calculate huge problems in their head but cannot light a fire properly. Their gifts are specific and not accompanied by others in any outstanding way. As often as possible, their gifts are use for entertainment only.

There is obvious value in trying to measure intelligence so that we can classify pupils as average, or above or below average and thus know what to expect of them. This is what we do when we weigh children and measure their height. It helps us to know what they should be capable of in physical work. Studies of intelligence have shown that it grows throughout childhood and adolescence, and this process of growth has led to idea of "mental age".

A child's intelligence "grows up" with him. But the rate of development may be different from his chronological increase in years. Thus a child of eight may be able to tackle mental activities which you would expect only from a ten year old. We say that this child has a "mental age" of ten, although his chronological age is only eight.

The ratio of mental age to chronological age expressed as a percentage has come to be one of the most important figures in the study of children's intelligence. It is called the intelligence quotient or I. Q. This is the standard rating for recording intelligence. Thus a child of eight with a mental age of ten turns out to have an I.Q. of 125, found thus:

$$\frac{\text{Mental age} \times 100}{\text{Chronological age}} = \frac{10 \times 100}{8} = 25$$

It should be obvious that a child with the same mental age and chronological age will have an I.Q. of 100. This is average intelligence. Like other physical qualities, both heredity and environment influence intelligence. It is affected by our state of health and emotional balance. But the most potent factor of environment is the amount of time the intelligence is used. Thus, the fullness of strength through exercise, which applies to the physical body, also applies to the mind.

Those children who grow up in homes, where the mind is stimulated develop mentally more than those from homes where there is no incentive to mental exercise. Likewise, those adults who take up jobs or cultural pursuits that constantly exercise the intellect maintain their standards of intelligence achieved in youth, whereas, those who spend their lives in routine, boring jobs or spend their leisure in ways, which make little or no call upon intelligence, actually decline in intelligence. There is a close analogy in the physical contrast between the strong, active man and the soft, obese fellow.

Heredity sets the limits of our intelligence; environment determines how near we got to these limits. But intelligence also has a strong effect upon a person socially. Extremely high intelligence tends to cut you off from people, because they cannot follow you in your interests. It has been reckoned that for leadership, an individual should have an I.Q. of about thirty points ahead of those he seeks to lead. Above this, the intellectual gap becomes too great, and below it, there is danger the followers will not recognise the superior qualities of the leader.

Children of High and Low Intelligence

The majority of all people are normal in size, but there are always some who are unusual, either because of their great size or extreme smallness. The same applies to intelligence. The majority of all people, adults, and children included, have an I.Q in the neighbourhood of hundred. But there are minority groups above one hundred and thirty and below seventy, who are like mental giants and deaf. These presents a problem, both to themselves and society, and as children, they should be of concern to the teacher.

The use of the term "mental age" can be misleading. Even when a child of nine can do the intellectual activities of a twelve year old, he is not just like an average twelve year old. He does not have the experience of the older child. On the other hand, he is much more creative and imaginative than the average twelve-year-old.

To say that mentally he is like a boy of twelve is like saying that a boy of fourteen years, who has grown unusually tall is a man. He is not. His proportions are all different, and his strength is not the same. So the teacher must be careful to remember when dealing with a child who is intellectually far advanced for his age, that he is not the same as an average child of older years but needs special attention. The same of course applies to a child of very low intelligence.

Highly gifted children should be nurtured because they could become the most valuable leaders in the society and are the kind of people whose intellect refreshes civilisation and pushes outwards the frontiers of knowledge. The fact that so few leaders do and that very few improve the culture of our civilisation is a dark reflection upon our schools and society, which have too often regarded the spirit of such youngsters as that of the wild horse — something to be broken before it can be used. Teaching such children demands special attention from the teacher to encourage and draw upon their talents and feed their appetites for fresh intellectual conquests.

The mentally dull child presents a challenge of another kind to the teacher. The sense of inferiority that such a child suffers at school, as he finds himself constantly overshadowed by the abilities of the other children, can fundamentally affect his character. In ordinary life, differences in intelligence do not appear in such vivid relief as they do in school, and so the teacher should concentrate on what the child can do, rather than constantly burden him with what he cannot do. No one would dream of making a dwarf a labourer, but many teachers give the mentally dull child the same mental burdens to carry as the normal child.

Instead, teachers should provide special light work for such children and turn their effort to helping them live well rather than learn well. Teachers should give the same kind of attention to those children as they do to the physically handicapped. Mental handicap is not the fault of the child, but results from pre-natal disorders, birth injuries and diseases. The sympathetic teacher can help such children to play a useful part in the community and help to prevent them from sinking, as so many do, into a life of delinquency and degradation.

The Exceptional Child (Handicapped and Gifted)

Characteristics and Needs
1. *Learning Disabilities*

Some children are not deaf but cannot understand language; some are not blind but cannot perceive visually; and some are not mentally retarded but cannot learn by conventional instruction methods. These children have specific learning disabilities.

The needs of these children are met in schools and in the society by reducing the environmental stimuli; by reducing the physical space in which the child works, play and lives; by simplifying the physical environment to reduce the number of choices; and by maximising the stimulus of the task of material.

2. Mental Retardation

Mentally retarded children are divided into four groups; the mildly retarded (IQ 55 to 69); the moderately retarded (IQ 40 to 54); the severely retarded (IQ25 to 39); and the profoundly retarded (IQ below 25).

Children with mild retardation do not grasp ideas, facts, or skills rapidly. They need repetition of the material taught, but they do learn and can use the content and skills taught in a regular school program. Moderately retarded children are unable to profit from regular methods of instruction but do have potential ability in three areas: academic subjects at a minimal level, social adjustment to the extent that the child can get along independently in the society, and occupational abilities to a degree the child can support himself or herself financially (partially or totally) as an adult.

The needs of these children are met through individual instruction in the academic areas; whole group participation in social fine arts, or physical education activities; and special occupational training in secondary school. The severely retarded child has only the potential for learning self-help skills; for social adjustment; and for economic usefulness in the home, in residential school, or in a sheltered workshop.

The profoundly retarded child is totally dependent on others for physical care, for socialisation, and for economic support. These individuals require complete care throughout their lives. Severely and profoundly retarded children are not usually placed in regular school settings.

3. Auditory and Hearing Disabilities

The age at which a child becomes deaf or develops a hearing loss has a significant influence on learning and schooling. A child who is born deaf or loses hearing before he or she learns to talk progresses much more slowly in speech and in understanding language. With improved hearing aids they can be taught in regular school, otherwise sign language is used.

4. Speech and Language Disorders

There are many forms of speech disorders: articulation, voice production, stuttering, retarded speech and speech disorders associated with deft palate, cerebral palsy, impaired hearing, and aphasia.

Speech therapists may teach the children once or twice a week. They also prepare assignments for teachers and parents to use to reinforce the skills taught by the therapist.

5. Visual Impairments

Total blindness is usually detected in a child before the age of one, but visual defects may remain undetected until the child enters school. Blind children are taught with special materials and can attend regular school, and also be provided with itinerant teachers or resource rooms.

6. Orthopaedic Problems

A child who is crippled or deformed or who has other physical handicaps has limited ability to cope with the academic and social experiences in a school setting. In the past, physically impaired children with mobility problems or manual dexterity problems were placed in special classes. Such placement caused the children problems of co-ordination, perception, and cognition as well as mobility.

Currently, physically handicapped children are place in a combination setting. They are placed in special classes with other handicapped children for games and activities that require little mobility and in regular classes with non-handicapped children so that they learn about the activities of normal children.

To accommodate orthopaedically handicapped children, school setting must include ramps, elevators, sturdy and steady equipment, handrails, wide halls, large classrooms, and bathrooms equipment with self-help aids.

Every child is entitled to an education wherein he can experience success — that which will enable him live a meaningful life. The role of the school system, therefore, is to provide conducive environment e.g. properly planned curriculum, teaching aid, well trained teachers, adequate infrastructure and facilities etc. that will make it possible for the child to experience success.

Based on this, handicapped children are also entitled to this right of early childhood education to enable them develop to that adult who do live a meaningful life. It is, therefore, proper to take care of their special needs by providing special education. By special education one means, the individually planned and systematically monitored arrangement of physical settings, special equipment and materials, teaching procedures and other interventions designed to help handicapped children achieve the greatest personal self-sufficiency and academic success. This means that the emphasis is on the individual child, and because each handicapped child is different, special interventions must be designed for him or her.

Handicapped children should be given an equal opportunity to develop physically, mentally and socially as being given to normal children, to make their own contribution to the society. They are not useless as many may believe. They have a place in the scheme of life just like any other person.

Gifted Child
This is an intellectually gifted child. There are many kinds of talented or gifted children with great differences among them. These children have potential IQs above 140 and represent about 1.33 percent of the population. These talents may be in social, mechanical, artistic, musical, physical, linguistic, and academic areas. The talented or gifted child may:

- Learn quickly and easily
- Reason, recognise relationships, and comprehend meanings
- Retain what was learnt
- Have a large vocabulary and use it accurately
- Ask many questions on many topics
- Be original in thought and methods
- Be keenly observant and respond quickly.

The needs of these children are met in various ways, including enrolment in special schools and classes. Enrichment is widely used in the elementary years. This is the provision of additional or more in-depth activities, materials and skills related to topics being taught. Administrative procedures include additional subjects, special teachers, and establishing higher standard of performance.

REFERENCES

Badmus, A. and Odediran, N.O. 2000. *A General Introduction to the Theory and Practice of Education.* Ilorin: Ahnour International.

Bernard, H.W. 1973. *Child Development and Learning.* Boston: Allyn & Bacon, Inc.

Blair, G.M., Jones, R.S. and Simpson, R.H. 1975. *Educational Psychology.* New York: Macmillan Publishing Co. Inc.

Deese, J. and Hulse, S.H. 1967. *The Psychology of Learning.* New York: McGraw - Hill Book Co.

Ekeruo, A.I.C. 1988. *Essentials of Educational Psychology.* Agbor: Central Books Nigeria Ltd.

Elkind, D. 1970. *Children and Adolescents: Interpretive Essays of Jean Piaget.* New York: Oxford University Press.

Erikson, E. 1963. *Childhood and Society.* New York: Norton.

Furth, H. 1970. *Piaget for Teachers.* Englewood Cliffs, N.J.: Prentice - Hall, Inc.

Hilgard, E.R. 1979. *Introduction to Psychology.* New York: Harcourt, Brace, Jovanovich Inc.

Hurlook, E.B. 1964. *Child Development.* New York: McGraw-Hill Book Co.

Mukherjee, A. 1978. *Educational Psychology.* Calcutta: K.P. Basu Publishing Co.

Oladele, J.O. 1989. *Fundamentals of Psychological Foundations of Education.* Lagos: John & Lad Publishers.

Chapter Five

IMPROVING CHILD EDUCATION

Does Anyone Really Care?

The tears of children being oppressed through abuse and neglect have become a torrent. The oppressive act of depriving the Nigerian children of their right to education in their early age has often made them feel that they have no help - that no one really cares about them.

Despite this torrent of tears, some people are unmoved by the suffering of these children. They turn blind eyes to their pains as if they are not part of our national development. As long as things are going relatively well for some people and their families, they are not concerned about the physical, mental and social development of other children. "Who cares?" One observer lamented the uncaring attitudes which has developed today in the Nigerian Society. The old philosophy and tradition of caring and sharing is being replaced by a new code of making and taking for ourselves only, with almost complete indifference to the plight of the children.

There surely is a need for someone to care for the proper development of the children as we think of how to improve the educational status of the Nigeria child. We all need to care if we really want to bring up children who will become responsible, dedicated and creative adults in the future. Our collective roles shall see us to the fulfilment of this goal.

Do our children ask too much of us? This is a question we can provide answer to ourselves and see that the children are simply asking for their rights of which education is one. Otherwise, what makes a good citizen? Training and developing the children early enough to be good, law abiding and productive for the benefit of the society.

Can Early Education Make a Difference?
For more than a decade, research on approaches to early childhood education has sought to investigate the effectiveness of various kinds of programmes in changing behaviour and enhancing development.

The results of these investigations have been disheartening. However, if some additional measures of school success is taken into account, research now indicates that early educational intervention can and does make a difference, very significantly. For example, it has turned out that the young adults who participated in some experimental programmes carried out in the 1960s failed few lessons while in school than those who did not participate in any such programmes.

This clearly indicates that early education can reduce the rate of failure for low-income children, thereby saving cost. There is an improved physical, mental and social interactions that bring out the skills mastered by the children for a better relationship with the society.

Schools
We must make schools as effective and efficient as they can be, to meet the task of developing and moulding the children.

Making the Best of the School
It costs a great deal of money to build and equip a modern school. But if the fact of limited budgets is accepted as a feature likely to be with us for a long time, we will be able to turn our thinking away from the bigger outlook of waiting until something is provided and develop a more positive self-help attitude. Once there is a willingness to do it yourself, it is possible to make changes in existing schools that will make all the difference between the rough and tumble down places so often found, and the clean, attractive schools that they might be.

Here is where the leadership qualities of the school head can play an active part. First, he must have an ideal towards which he aims, remembering that a well-organised, good looking, and well kept school is an environment for all who use it, which affects positively their tastes, morale, happiness, and behaviour.

Spheres in which improvements can often be made are:

1. *The Grounds*

When building a new school, ideally the land should be spacious, well drained and flat, so that building is cheap and the compound games is filled. Farm and gardens can also be easily laid out. In practice, if the school is already built on rough ground, the best that can be done to provide satisfactory play grounds and game pitches is to choose the most suitable land nearby and clear it and level it before marking out for particular games or other needs. For games, short grasses should be encouraged. The whole area occupied by the school and its grounds should be hedged with a suitable plant for keeping out unwanted animals. This can be attractive as well as effective, so much the better.

The most important, however, whether the area is small or large, is to keep the grounds neat and tidy. Keep the grass well cut and the play ground free from litter and rubbish. Flower beds provide a colourful and attractive contribution to the appearance of the grounds, but they need constant care. Beautiful colour can also be provided for the environment by planting flowering trees and shrubs.

Some of the most beautiful ornamental gardens of the ancient world were in Africa. Why can't we bring back the practice of that culture of beautifying our environment, which could be another source of joy to us all?

2. *The Buildings*

There is nothing that can be done about the shape size or orientation of a school once it has been built, but there is much that can be done about how its accommodation is used and its appearance is cared for. Too many teachers seem unconcerned about the leaky roofs and dirty crumbling walls. The least they can do is to report the repairs that are needed. But a little effort and ingenuity can change the darkness of the average school into the trim, businesslike place it could be.

Wastage always results from careless usage. It goes on in many schools despite the knowledge that funds are low. It is good to look after what we have. The teachers and the pupils/students have to develop the habit of looking after all school property with as much care as they do their own.

Storage should be adequate, not only for the teachers, their equipment and materials, but also for the children. Much of the property untidiness in schools is the result of insufficient storage space.

Table 5.1: Ornamental Trees and Flowering Shrubs

NAME	DESCRIPTION	FLOWERING PERIOD
Flamboyant or flame of the forest	Large bright red flowers precede the leaves	End of dry season
Pink Bauhinia	Flat-topped, wide spreading, pink flowers precedes the pale green leaves	End of dry season
Jacaranda	Tall, slender tree; masses of blue flowers formed at the ends of branches, followed by dark green feathery leaves	Dry season and beginning of rain
Pink Cassia	Shapeless at first, developing into an attractive tree with a rounded crown; masses of sweet-scented pink blossom produced with the new foliage	Beginning of wet season
Horse Cassia	Remains green throughout the dry seasons; dark yellow clusters of flowers formed at end of branches among the dark green leaves	Middle of rain
Tullip Tree (E. Africa Flame tree)	Dark green leaves which fall in the dry season, large upright orange flowers	End of rain

Tecoma Stans	Yellow clusters of trumpet-shaped flowers, pointed pale green leaves which fall in dry weather	Middle of rains
Allamanda	Yellow trumpet-shaped, flowers, dark evergreen leaves	All year round
Bougainvillaea	a. Purple flowers, small green leaves b. Red flowers, large dark green leaves; climbs and needs support	Masses in dry seasons but flowers year round
Duranta	Blue-mauve flowers at the end of branches produce orange berries; pale green leaves fall in dry weather	Wet season
Hibiscus	Various colours, red most common; some double varieties; green leaves all year	All year round
Gamboge	Narrow pale green leaves, yellow bell-shaped flowers; very hardy green all year	Wet season
Plumbago	Page green leaves, blue flower	All year round, but prolific in dry season
Pride of Barbados	Orange of yellow flowers small pale green leaves	End of rains

Curriculum

Good curriculum must be planned with definite objectives and purpose in mind. Evidence is mounting that formulating and carrying a specific plan for the pre-school programmes is fundamental to success, at least when working with economically disadvantaged children.

An aspect of planning that deserves special consideration is that curriculum should be comprehensive in coverage. A valuable way to think about this is to picture the child as being composed of a number of selves, as mentioned earlier: the physical self; the emotional self, the social self, the creative self and the cognitive self. These five selves succeed in covering the personality of the child.

One way of assuring that the curriculum is both comprehensive and purposeful is to discipline oneself (as a teacher) by filling out the Curriculum Analysis Chart each week, to be certain there is something deliberately planned for each "self" of the child everyday to purposely enhance his or her growth. Another more in-depth way of planning curriculum involves the use of a Daily Plan Chart where the provision of more detail is possible.

Table 5.2: Curriculum Analysis Chart for the teacher

Part of self being Developed	Mon.	Tues.	Wed	Thus	Fri.	Special Notes
Physical self						Nature of activity
						Specific purpose value for child
Emotional Self: mental health						Nature of Activity
						Specific purpose value for child
Social Self						Nature of Activity
						Specific purpose value for child
Social self: multicultural and non-existing emphasis						Nature of activity
						Specific purpose value for child
Creative self						Nature of activity
						Specific purpose value for child
Cognitive self						Nature of activity
						Specific purpose value for child
Cognitive self Language						Nature of activity
						Specific purpose value for child

A good curriculum programme must have stability and regularity combined with flexibility. Young children need to know what is likely to happen next during the day.

This means that the order of events should be generally predictable. Predictability enables the child to prepare mentally for the next event; it makes compliance with routines more likely and helps children feel secure.

A good programme of a curriculum must have variety. Children need many different kinds of experiences as well as changes in basic experiences. Many teachers think of variety of experience in terms of field trips or covering different topics, such as families or baby animals. But another kind of variety that should also be considered is variety in every day basic learning experience. What is different there is between the school that has the same pet rat and bowl of goldfish all year round and two snakes as visitors. Lack of variety doesn't supply the variety of experiences needed to stimulate the child.

Children should be offered various levels of difficulty in activity materials. Materials that are challenging must be provided for all ages. The programmes of the curriculum should become more challenging and move from simple to more complex activities as the year progresses and the children mature and gain competence. The school curriculum should not look the same in May, for instance, as it did in September.

Children need changes of peace during the day to avoid monotony and fatigue and to maintain a balance of kinds of experiences for them. The most obvious way to incorporate variation of pace is to plan for it in the overall schedule. For example, a quiet snack can be followed by a dance period.

Learning must be based on actual experience and participation. Children learn best if allowed to use all their senses as avenues of learning. Participatory experience is an essential ingredient in early childhood learnings; real experiences with real things, rather than limited to the verbal discussions and pictures commonly used.

Another long held value in early childhood education is an appreciation of play as a facilitator of learning. Play is the medium used by children to translate experience into something internally meaningful to them.

Schools should be full of pleasure to both children and teachers. Experience of pleasure; humour and laughter, should be very much a part of each school day.

The setting of a good school is established with children in mind; furniture is made to the right size; the building has easy access to the yard; and there is a general air of orderliness, yet, easy comfortable and beautiful. This kind of atmosphere goes a long way toward making parents feel at home and part of the school family. Other facilities such as library, clinic, computer games, motion pictures, video, television, radio, tape recorder etc in good condition will aid in the improvement of the development of the children. Qualified staff strength and dynamic administration provide conducive atmosphere devoid of confusion for effective teaching and learning.

Table 5.3: National Summary of Primary School Statistics (1988 - 1994)

	1988	1989	1990	1991	1992	1993	1994
Total Schools	33796	34904	35433	35446	36610	38254	38649
Total Enrolments	12690789	12721087	13607249	13776854	14805937	15870280	16190947
Total Male Enrolment	7308218	6997356	7729677	7741897	8273824	8930600	9056367
	57.59%	56.01%	56.81%	56.19%	55.88%	56.27%	55.93%
Total Female Enrolment	5382580	5723731	5877572	6034957	6532113	6939680	7134580
	42.41%	44.99%	43.81%	43.81%	44.12%	43.73%	44.07%
Total Teacher	308178	344221	331915	353600	384212	428097	435210
Total Male Teacher	204178	190979	189499	202753	211650	236266	233305
	66.25%	55.48%	57.09%	57.34%	55.09%	55.19%	53.61%
Total Female Teacher	104004	153242	142416	150847	172562	191831	201905
	33.75%	44.52%	42.91%	42.66%	44.91%	44.81%	46.39%
Total Classrooms		375726	376611	377439	407789	447859	444985
Teacher pupil ratio	1:41	1:37	1:36	1:37	1:39	1:37	1:37

Source: Statistics Branch, F.M.E. May 1995

Table 5:4: National Summary of Post-Primary School Statistics (1984/85-1994)

	1984/85	1986	1987	1988	1989	1990	1991	1992	1993	1993
Total No. of School	5927	5819	6092	5991	5868	6001	5860	6009	5959	6071
Total Enrolment	22988174	3088711	2934349	2941791	2723791	2901993	3123277	3600620	4032083	44513
Total Male Enrolment	757035	1758866	1700222	1729637	1581648	1661468	1821307	1979045	2182034	24197
	58.80%	56..94%	57.94%	58.79%	58.07%	57.25%	58.31%	54.96%	54.0%	54..0%
Total Female Enrolment	1231139	1329845	1329845	1212244	1142143	1240525	1301970	1621575	1850049	20315
	41.20%	43.06%	42.06%	41.21%	41.93%	42.75%	41.69%	45.04%	46.0%	46.0%
Total No of Teachers	105003	82021	135034	134400	135677	141377	141491	147530	151722	15259
Total Male Teachers	75101	57063	96434	92443	92976	95303	96555	96103	99359	97647
	7152%	69.57%	70.67%	67.8%	80.3%	67.41%	68.24%	66.5%	65.0%	64.0%
Total Female Teachers	29902	57063	39600	41957	43701	46074	44936	49427	52363	54949
	28.48%	69.57%	29.33%	31.33%	31.97%	32.59%	31.76%	32.5%	35.05%	36.0%
Total No of Classrooms	-	-	-	-	-	-	82930	90494	104693	10092
Teacher Student Ratio	1:29	1:38	1:22	1:22	1:20	1:21	1:22	1:25	1:29	1:29

Source: Statistics Branch, F.M.E, May 1995

1995 Primary School Statistics Indications

1. Number of Primary Schools = 41,531

2. Total Primary School Enrolment:
Boys	Girls
8,729,421	7,011,657

   = 15,741,078

   (55.5%)   (44.5%)

3. Number of Primary School Teacher:
   (M)   (F)
   230,827   207,332   = 437,619
4. Teacher/Pupils Ratio   = 1:36

1996 Post-primary School Statistical Indicators

1. Number of Post-Primary Schools = 64291
2. Student Enrolment by levels
   Junior Secondary School (JS I - III)

Boys	**Girls**		
1,441,270	1,287,461	=	2,728,731
(52.8%)	(47.2%)		

   Senior Secondary School (SS I - III)

Boys	**Girls**		
913,443	806,817	=	1,720,260
(53.1%)	(46.9%)		

3. Total Students' Enrolment (JS I - III)

Boys	**Girls**		
2,354,713	2,094,279	=	4,448,991
(52.9%)	(47.1%)		

4. Post-Primary School Teachers:

(M)	(F)		
100,956	57,166	=	158,122
(63.8%)	(36.2%)		

5. Teacher/Students Ratio = 1:28
6. Classroom/Students Ratio = 1:41

Table 5.5: 1995 Primary School Enrolment by State and Sex

STATE	MALE	FEMALE	TOTAL
Abia	241,135	241,221	482,356
Adamawa	280,732	215,316	496,048
Akwa Ibom	322,943	326,858	649,801
Anambra	207,229	201,857	409,086
Bauchi	275,423	176,630	452,053
Benue	390,202	289,892	680,094
Borno	351,824	249,541	601,365
Cross River	119,956	115,298	235,254

Delta	214,460	236,326	450,786
Edo	240,000	267,020	507,020
Enugu	331,867	296,881	628,748
Imo	286,816	274,398	561,214
Jigawa	236,982	122,705	359,687
Kaduna	307,805	223,206	531,011
Kano	510,606	308,216	818,822
Katsina	431,197	205,416	636,613
Kebbi	137,723	67,916	205,639
Kogi	255,939	222,547	478,486
Kwara	166,354	149,226	315,580
Lagos	430,315	429,529	859,844
Niger	256,751	152,291	409,042
Ogun	237,820	220,515	458,335
Ondo	297,518	285,473	582,991
Osun	313,794	296,971	610,765
Oyo	370,845	369,987	740,832
Plateau	405,049	314,296	719,345
Rivers	294,886	298,615	593,501
Sokoto	233,498	73,705	307,203
Taraba	241,949	175,984	417,933
Yobe	283,168	160,268	443,436
FCT, Abuja	52,630	45,553	98,183
NIGERIA	8,729,421	7,011,657	15,744,078

Table 5.6: 1995 Post-Primary School Enrolment by State and Sex

STATE	MALE	FEMALE	TOTAL
Abia	73,385	78,268	141,806
Adamawa	36,594	21,681	58,275
Akwa Ibom	80,331	82,391	162,722
Anambra	62,653	92,640	155,293
Bauchi	61,925	36,088	97,933
Benue	102,238	51,088	153,326
Borno	41,170	33,725	74,895
Cross River	46,814	44,387	91,201
Delta	118,928	125,446	244,376
Edo	98,637	113,379	212,016
Enugu	53,223	78,444	131,667
Imo	70,319	115,707	186,026
Jigawa	15,448	8,585	24,033
Kaduna	77,999	58,056	136,055
Kano	64,168	40,803	104,971
Katsina	42,605	16,562	59,167
Kebbi	21,060	5,874	26,934
Kogi	65,629	45,271	110,900
Kwara	62,636	54,061	116,697
Lagos	283,716	304,438	588,154
Niger	79,136	38,261	117,397
Ogun	100,493	93,868	194,361
Ondo	87,451	86,637	174,088
Osun	11,466	99,301	210,767
Oyo	169,284	155,442	324,727
Plateau	100,681	65,900	166,581
Rivers	112,012	101,830	213,842
Sokoto	36,537	11,578	49,641
Taraba	36,537	13,104	49,641
Yobe	9,844	13,104	12,726
FCT, Abuja	26,298	16,650	42,948
NIGERIA	**2,354,715**	**2,094,276**	**4,448,991**

Teachers

The most important person who helps the children adjust to a school environment is the teacher. Teaching young children needs well adjusted, intelligent, enlighten, energetic, and creative teachers. Such teachers will see teaching as a challenging and satisfying career. Those who like talkative, inquisitive children will find teaching children exciting, demanding and rewarding.

Training

Teaching children should not be regarded as simply a part-time job, or an unsupervised play situation. It is a highly professional occupation and as such, those going into it should be well-trained and committed persons. Their professional preparation does not end with a college or university degree, but there is a constant need for continuous re-education through in-service programmes, conferences, and professional seminars, to add to their knowledge about children and how to develop them. No person should contemplate teaching without realising that professional growth will never end.

Attitude

If all the messy things children do; their slowness, reluctance, forgetfulness bother you, then teaching young children is not for you. To be with young children daily, week after week, you must be interested in things that crawl and a few that don't; find satisfaction in teaching children to do little things; and have patience while they paint themselves as well as their paper. To go through all this, the teacher must be gentle but firm, patient and encouraging, comforting yet demanding.

Appearance

A teacher who is satisfied with his or her job is always beautiful to the children. To the children, beauty is a pleasant personality, comforting nature, and bright cheerful clothing. An interested and committed teacher will consider all the messy activities and occurrences and dress accordingly.

Since teaching is an active, rather than a passive activity, clothing must be suitable for bending, crawling, sitting, and getting into things. The teacher is an active participant in all the children's activities as well as an observer.

Role

One important role of a teacher is to establish a physical, social, emotional and intellectual environment where children can learn to function in a group setting.

The second role is the teacher being a good planner of programme. He or she must do the selecting and developing of goals and objectives of classroom programme, which are converted to activities that are right for the needs of the children.

The teacher must develop a systematic method of evaluating and recording each child's performance towards achieving the set goals. It is from this evaluation that the teacher is capable of individualising the activities to meet each child's need in his or her learning process.

The third role is the teacher as a classroom manager, in which he or she organises and arranges classroom activities and materials, maintaining controlled classroom according to policies established for schools.

The fourth role is that of a liaison between school and parents through arranging for home visits, special programmes, conferences, parents observation visits, and early introductory sessions for parents and children. Children intending to attend a school should be arranged to visit the school with their parents to familiarise themselves with the school setting.

The fifth role is that of a representative of the children and parents, as well as a representative of the programme of the school. As a staff of the school, he or she understands the programme of the school and passes them to parents and teachers.

Apart from being a teacher of young children, there should be other career opportunities in the field of education for teachers. Teachers should be given the opportunity of upgrading their qualifications, becoming more professional in order to climb the career ladder in the field of education. The Federal, State, even Local Government and Ministry of Education should have career positions for those teachers who have, over the years, become experienced, committed professionals in teaching. Such enriched minds in children education will help in modifying the policies and curriculum of schools to fit in with the moving time, thereby making them dynamic, producing improved results in achieving the set educational goals.

The colleges and universities should provide opportunities for teachers of young children, who have improved their professionalism, to help train those who are interested in becoming teachers of early childhood education. There should be an aspect of specialisation in this case. These degree holders will help in the improvement of the practice of the profession. For these individuals, administrative and supervisory positions must be available.

Special resource teachers may act as consultants to teachers in various capacities such as, directors of parents' activities, health and nutritional experts, and social workers. Education counsellor is another important position a teacher, who had been through with the psychological, sociological and physiological development of children, can occupy in schools. In this aspect, advice is given on "child development".

Aide is another position in school a teacher can take to complement the effort of the classroom teacher. In this position, he or she is seconded to the classroom teacher with responsibilities that help not only the teacher, but also the children.

The teacher and the aide work hand in hand, for a successful implementation of the programme. An aide is not usually responsible for the initial instruction of skills or content, but assists in the follow-up activities or experiences that occur after the teacher has taught or presented the lessons. Because of this, it is important that the aide be included in the daily planning session, so that the goals of the lesson are known by both teacher and aide.

Those with lower qualification like Teachers Grade II certificate may start with this position, and from there, move up the career ladder. This provides practical experience opportunity with which to grow in the profession.

These career opportunity movement will encourage those who are interested in teaching young children to go into the profession. It provides teachers with the hope to grow better in life, thereby becoming committed to the profession as a full time job. Only such attitude can bring out the best from our educational system.

The Teacher's Roles

Just as schools are commonly accepted as a necessary part of education, so too is the teaching profession. If teachers are to do their job properly, they must come like the great teachers of the past with the fire of conviction that what they have to teach is important, and they must come with the loving attitude of a father to his children. The teacher's relationship with the pupils must be worked out by proving his concern for his pupils and not just their work. This cordial relationship will help him know from the children their natural eagerness to learn and direct it, not just to those things that interest them, but also to those things that are important. He must remain himself a pupil, ever learning more about his work.

For teachers to do a comprehensive job, they must see the child as a complex human being composed of many attributes and aspects, and they must see teaching as stimulating and enhancing the development of all these aspects. Good human relationships are a fundamental ingredient of a good day teaching.

Warmth and empathic understanding have been shown to be effective means of influencing young children's positive adjustment to school. And it is apparent that genuine caring about the children and other adults in the programme is fundamental to success. Person to person, one to one encounters are necessary.

The discipline of the teacher to adhere to the curriculum to achieve its purpose is of utmost importance. The teacher should be able to know each child well in order to plan activities that fit the individual child. The most significant value a teacher can convey to children is the conviction that school is satisfying fun by way of giving them pleasurable experiences.

The teacher should act as health-screen. He should make a health check (physical) of every child as he arrives at school each day. The teacher who sees the same children every day get to know how they usually look and behave and can often spot such variations promptly and thus avoid exposing other children in school to the condition. The teacher must know what to do when a child becomes ill at school. Teachers must never forget that the children in their care are not their own and that supervising them carries with it a special responsibility. General health precautions should be observed by children and staff (teachers).

Teachers need to be able to recognise these stages of development so they can adjust their activities, offering to provide a good balance between opportunities for practice in order to consolidate the skill and opportunities for accepting the challenge of a slightly more difficult activity to go on. During outdoor playtime at the pre-primary level, the teachers are required to actively be involved with the children by observing and being alert to ways to make the play richer. The teacher needs to keep the environment safe.

Some Personal Qualities that will Help the Teacher Establish a Therapeutic Climate in the Nursery School

Early childhood teachers should utilise their personal qualities, as well as, what is commonly referred to as teaching techniques to foster a therapeutic, growth enhancing climate for young children. These qualities are as discussed below.

Consistency
One way to build a sense of trust between teachers and children is to behave in ways children can predict and to be consistent about maintaining guidelines and schedules; a very basic form of being trustworthy and dependable. Thus the children know what to expect and do not live in fear of erratic or temperamental responses to what they do. For this reason, emotional stability is a highly desirable trait for teachers of young children to possess.

Reasonableness
That is, the teacher is neither expecting too much nor too little from the children. Learning the characteristics of child developmental stages will help the teacher on this.

Courage and Strength of Character
When dealing with or outbursts anger in particular, the teacher will find that courage and strength of character are required to see such outbursts through. The teacher doesn't have to placate any angry child or, allow him or her to run off or have his or her way.

Trustfulness and Confidence
This is, the teacher's faith that the child wants to grow and develop in a healthy way. Children respond to what is genuinely expected of them by the people who matter to them. Consequently, the children will always respond to the teacher's good intention for them.

Empathy
This is the ability to feel as another person feels, to feel with him; rather than feel for him. This allows teacher to put himself in the child's place, as it helps him identify and clarify for the child, how he or she is feeling.

Warmth
The warm teacher lets the children and staff know that he likes them and thinks well of them. Both children and adults flourish in this climate of sincere approval and acceptance.

Appreciation
The teacher must be able to take time to relish and enjoy the children in their care. Appreciation is compounded of perceptive understanding and empathy.

Practical Things the Teacher Can Do to Help Young Children Achieve Healthy, Emotional Development

Children are resilient. They bounce back from their own and others' mistakes, and it is unlikely that one imperfect handling of a situation will inflict permanent damage on a child. The teacher therefore should not be unduly hesitant on the grounds that he may injure the child. The teacher should do the following things:

Develop Friendly, Close Relationship with Each Family:
If the school and family establish a feeling of closeness and shared interest in the child's welfare, it is easier for her to make this transition, since her world is thereby widened rather than split into two pieces.

Reduce Frustration for the Child When Possible
Children should not have to spend time waiting for things to happen. Children's needs are immediate, intense and personal, and the longer they are kept waiting, the more irritable they become. Snack should be available as the children sit down and some one should be outside for supervision as the children are dressed and ready to go out to play.

Duplicates of equipment mean that there is generally enough to go round, two or three toy tracks are much more satisfactory than just one.

A good assortment of activities must be available so that three-year-old children are not expected to stack tiny plastic blocks and five-year-old children do not have to make do with eight-year-old children's piece puzzles. The day should be planned, so that few and moderate demands are made on children at points where they are likely to be tired and hungry.

Learn to Identify and Describe the Children's Feelings to them and Help them Express these Feelings to the Relevant People
In our society, we seem to have reached the conclusion that it is dangerous to allow some emotions to be expressed. The assumption being that, if they are expressed, they will become stronger or the person will act the feeling out, but if we ignore them or deny their presence they will vanish.

Actually, the opposite of this premise is psychologically true. A poem from William Blake's "A Poison Tree" puts this neatly:

> I was angry with my friend
> I told my wrath, my wrath did end
> I told it not, my wrath did grow.

Negative emotions that are recognised, accepted and expressed usually fade, but if not expressed, they seem to generate pressure that causes the person to release them ultimately in a more explosive or veiled, yet hostile way.

Also if children are not provided with ways of telling others how they feel, they are almost inevitably drawn to show how they feel by acting the feelings out. The advantage of helping the child to know how he feels is not only that we avoid these overwhelming explosion or complicated emotions displacement, but he also learns that emotions are acceptable, therefore, an important part of himself is acceptable. As he matures, this self-knowledge forms a foundation for learning to express feeling in a way that harms neither himself nor other people.

Learn to Recognise Signs of Stress and Emotional upset in Children
Children give many signals besides crying or fussing that indicate emotional stress. Reverting (regressing) to less mature behaviour is a common signal. We are all familiar with the independent four years old who suddenly

wants to be babied while recovering from the flu or the child who wets his bed after the babies arrive. Various nervous habits such as hair twisting, sighing deeply, nail biting or thumb sucking, also reveal that the child is under stress.

Know What to do for Children Who are Emotionally Upset
Emotional upsets have to be handled on a short-term basis and sometimes on a long-term basis as well. On short term emergency treatment, the first thing to do for a child who is upset to the point of fear is to comfort him or her. But the manner of comfort will vary from child to child. Find out what is causing the child the emotional upset.

Teaching Methods
The school child has to be taught in activities that will develop his or her physical, mental and social selves, which make up the whole child who becomes an adult in the future. The teaching methods must, therefore, be those activities, which focus on developing these selves to get the best out of the child.

Table 5.7: Age at Which a Given Percentage of Children Perform Locomotor Skills

	25 %	50%	75%	90%
Roll over	2.3mo	2.8 mo	3.8 mo	4.7 mo
Sits without support	4.8mo	5.5 mo	6.5 mo	7.9 mo
Walks well	11.3 mo	12.1 mo	13.5 mo	14.3 mo
Kicks ball forward	15 mo	20 mo	22.3 mo	2 yrs
Pedals bike	21 mo	23.9 mo	2.8 yrs	3 yrs
Balances on one foot (10 secs)	3 yrs	4.5 yrs	5 yrs	6.9 yrs
Hops on one foot	3 yrs	3.4 yrs	4 yrs	4.9 yrs
Catches bounded ball	3.5 yrs	3.9 yrs	4.9 yrs	5.5 yrs
Heel-to-toe walk	3.3.yrs	3.6 yrs	4.2 yrs	5 yrs

Development of the Physical Self

The educational implications of this development principle for early childhood teachers are that school children need ample opportunities to use their large muscles in vigorous, energetic, physical play. It can be tormenting for young children to have to remain confined too long on chairs and behind tables.

However, since the finer muscle, eye-hand skills are also beginning to develop during this period, activities that stimulate the children to practice these skills should also be offered, but not overdone so that excessive demands are made on the children's self control.

Good food, reasonable toilet procedures, and adequate rest are important factors in maintaining the physical and emotional well being of young children. Additional factors that affect the physical development of children include health and safety, and provision of maximum opportunities for their bodies to grow and develop in the healthiest way. These could be:

1. *Promotion of Health and Safety in the Nursery School*

This is very important, and could be achieved by ways of encouraging parents to make sure their children have regular health check-ups and immunisations. The parent should be required to present to the school up-to-date immunisation records, and physical examinations should be required too before the child enrols. Such certification not only protects the child in question, but all the other children and adults in the school as well.

2. *Fostering Large Muscle Development in Young Children*

In general, the school should furnish a large assortment of big, sturdy, durable equipment that provides many opportunities for all kinds of physical activity, and it should also provide a teacher who values vigorous large muscle play and who encourage the children to participate freely in this pleasure. Equipment good for crawling through, climbing up, balancing on, and hanging from, should be included.

The children will need things they can lift, haul, and shove around to test their strength and use to make discoveries about physical properties the equipment possess. They need things they can use for construction and they provide opportunities for rhythmic activities, such as bouncing, jumping and swinging. In addition, there must be places of generous size for them to carry out the wonderful sensory experiences that involve mud, sand, and water. Finally, they need plenty of space in which to simply move about.

3. Fostering Sensory Integration and Experience

Sensory integration is one of the most basic aspects of physical development. The senses of seeing, hearing, touch, smell and taste must be integrated and experienced in activities designed for such. All these senses and systems require stimulation in order to develop adequately and operate effectively together, and this sensory integration is vital for later development.

Since sensory integration is a very basic neurological process, early stimulation is particularly valuable. The teacher's focus should not be only on developing the children's skills, but also on providing a series of experiences designed to bring about such integration. For example, such activities as stroking a child's body with various textures, having the children roll about inside a carpeted cylinder etc.

4. Use of Perceptual-motor Activities to Enhance Physical Development

There are two ways to approach the areas of planned perceptual motor activities; the first provides opportunities for practice in specific skills, and the second uses physical activity to promote creative thought and self-expression. Both approaches have merits. Perceptual motor activities do not require children to be regimented and drilled, they are easy body movements. They can be divided into the following categories: locomotion, balance, body and space perception, rhythm and temporal awareness, rebound and airborne activities, projectile management, management of daily motor activities and tension releasers. Repeated practice in each of the categories are necessary. See Table 5.8

Table 5.8: Categories of Physical Activities and Some Suggestions for Providing Practice of these Skills at the Pre-school

Category	Illustration	Comment
Locomotion rolling	Roll over and over; sideways, both directions. Forward roll (somersault)	Nice to have tumbling mats, but not essential, rug, grass, or clean floor also work
Crawling/creeping	Move by placing weight on elbows only, dragging feet. Crawl, using arm and leg in unison, on the same side of the body or use alternating arm/legs crawl	Work well to give animal movements
Climbing	Apparatus valuable here good to incorporate stretching, hanging and reaching in this activity	Necessary to be careful of safety
Walking	Can vary with big, little steps, fast or slow. Encourage movement in different directions	Good to do walking activities bare-foot on contrasting surfaces for sensory input
Stair climbing	Nice to use this during an excursion, unless nursery school has a five to six step stairway	This is an interesting indicator of developmental level: young children take steps, one at a time, drawing second foot up to meet leading foot. Older children alternate feet in this task
Jumping, hopping, and skipping	Children can jump over lines or very low obstacles, as well as jump down from blocks of various heights. Hopping is difficult for young children, it is a prelude to skipping. Encourage learning	Can use animal names here also

	to hop on either foot and alternative feet. Skipping is often too difficult Valuable skill to ultimately acquire, since it involves crossing midline in a rhythmical alternating pattern	
Running and leaping	Nice to find large, grassy area for these kinds of activities, makes a nice field trip	Don't encourage running backward, young children often catch feet and trip themselves
Static balance (Balance while still)	Balance lying on side. Balance standing on tiptoes	Often provides emotional relief too. Gives marvellous feeling of freedom, power and satisfaction
	Balance on one foot, then the other, for short period of time	
Dynamics (Balance while moving)	Use balance beam many ways, or use large hollow blocks as "stepping stones", or walk on lines build a beam that tapers from wide to narrow for the children to use	It is a particularly challenging task; may overwhelm some children
Balance using an object	Balance beanbags on hands, or back, or head. Work with unbalanced objects pole with weight on one end, for example, movement education techniques apply to this category particularly well	
Body and space perception	How big can you be? How little? Can you make a "sad" face: Can you fit inside this circle? Can you fill up this (a very big one)?	Helps to refer to other people's bodies, for example, where is Henry's elbow?

	How much of you can you get in the air at once? Use shadow dancing for effective awareness building	Listening, imitative actions such as "Simon says" are fun if not practised for too long
	Any movement to music or to a rhythmic beat. Can be varied in many ways; fast, slow, or with different rhythmic patterns. Important, simple and clear with pre-schoolers	Can stress position in space, "over", "under", and so on: tedious if overdone Creative dance is the usual medium — "rhythm band" is typical.
Rebounding and air borne activities	In nursery schools, these are generally thought of as "bouncing" activities; mattresses, bouncing boards; and large inner tubes offer various levels of difficulty. Swings and hand-over hand bars are also in a sense, air borne	
Project management: throwing and catching	Throwing and catching usually require teachers' participation Children throw best using relatively small objects but catch best using large ones	The problem is to use objects that move slowly enough and harmless: nerf balls, large rubber balls, and fleece balls beanbags, meet this requirement.
	Can throw objects at target such as wall, or into large box For catching, older children can use pitch-back net; useful for understanding the effect of force in relation to throwing Begins with kicking a "still" ball, then goes onto a gently rolling one	
Kicking	Hit balloons with hands and then with paddle	Need lots of bean bags; not much fun to have to run and pick them up after every two or three throws

Bouncing	Can hit ball balanced on traffic cone with able light plastic bat	
Daily motor activities (fine muscle activities)	Best with large, rubber ball, use two hands and then progress to one hand; bounce to other children	Many teacher are nervous about striking activities, but these activities are challenging to children and worth the careful supervision and rule setting they require
	Includes many self-help skills, such as, buttoning and even tooth brushing! Also include the use of almost all self-expressive materials, and use of tools in carpentry and cooking	
Tension releasers and relaxation techniques	See discussion on fine muscle activities in text	Be careful of over fatigue

The second aspect of perceptual motor activities is relaxation and tension relieving activities. Sometimes, we do not think of relaxation as being a motor skill. However, the ability to relax and let go can be learned, and the ever increasing stress of life as people mature in our culture make acquiring these techniques invaluable. Tension, of course, is intimately tied to emotional states as well as to activity level.

Using Physical Activity to Promote Creative Thought and Self-expression
One of the newer aspects of creative physical education is termed Movement Education. It is a nice blend of physical activity and problem solving that can be considerable fun for children.

For instance, the teacher may ask a child, "is there some way you could get across the rug without using your feet?" It is obvious how this kind of teaching fosters the development of fluency in ideas.

Movement education also contributes to knowing more about the body being aware of various parts and how they work together.

Another aspect of creative physical education is using creative dance as a means of self-expression. Dancing can be the freest and most joyful of all large motor activities. For young children, dancing usually means moving rhythmically to music in a variety of relatively constructed ways. The teacher who sets out to teach the children specific patterns of dancing, surely limits the creative aspects of this experience. What works best is to have an array of records or tapes on hand with which the teacher is very familiar and which provide a selection of moods and temperament, dancing, this surely increase the creative aspects of this experience.

By using this comprehensive approach, teachers can assure themselves that physical development of the child is being facilitated to its fullest potential.

Fostering Mental Health
Early childhood programme can make valuable contributions to fostering mental health of the children, by presenting outstanding opportunities for carrying out preventive and remedial work in this area.

In an era when at least one in every ten people is destined to spend time in a mental hospital and where the World Health Organisation (WHO, 1997) reports the prevalence of persistent and socially handicapping mental health problems among children as being between 15-20% in developing countries, the importance of such work is clear. And we must give careful consideration to practical things teachers must do that are likely to foster mental health in the children in their care.

Importance of Developing Basic Attitudes of Trust, Autonomy, Initiative, Accomplishment and Identity
The most fundamental thing the teacher can do to foster mental health in young children is to provide many opportunities for basic healthy emotional attitudes to develop.

Early childhood encompasses five basic stages of emotional development in which these attitudes are formed.

These stages are:

1. *Trust v. Mistrust*
The child learns, or fails to learn, that other people can be depended on

and also that he can depend on himself to elicit needed responses to them. This stage starts from the home with parents. Therefore, it is vital that the basic climate of the school encourage the establishment of trust between everyone who is part of the school community.

2. *Autonomy v. Shame and Doubt*

These attitudes are formed during the same period in which toilet training takes place. During this time, the child is acquiring the skills of holding on and letting go. This fundamental exercise in self-assertion and control is associated with the child's drive to become independent and to express this independence by making choices and decisions. Children who are over regulated and deprived of the opportunity to establish independence and autonomy may become oppressed with feelings of shame and self doubt, which result in losing self esteem, being defiant, trying to get away with things, and in later life in developing various forms of compulsive behaviour. The desirable way to handle this strong need for choice and self-assertion is to provide an environment at home and school, that makes many opportunities available for the child to do for himself and to make decision.

3. *Initiative v. Guilt*

Around the age of 4 or 5 and above, he becomes more interested in reaching out to the world around him, in doing things, and in being part of the group. At this stage, he wants to think things up and try them out; he is interested in the effect his actions have on other people; and he becomes an avid seeker of information about the world around him. By encouraging the child's ability to initiate plans and take action will enhance the child's feeling of self worth and creativity as well as his ability to be a self-starter all highly desirable outcomes necessary for future development and happiness.

4. *Accomplishment v. Inferiority*

At this stage, children want to be involved in real tasks that they can complete. After a period of fantasy and imagination, they want to learn exactly how to do things and how to do them well.

5. The Sense of Identity
This stage is usually reached during adolescence when children are seeking to clarify who they are and what their future roles in society are to be.

These stages have to be studied and mastered by the teachers in order to make sure the emotional development of the children is completely fulfilled. Since these psychological stages motivate the behaviour of children, teachers must take them into account in planning programmes and activities, selecting materials and equipment, understanding and accepting normal behaviour.

Emotional Traits to Check in the Child
To determine whether the child is in good emotional health, the teacher should ask the following questions about the child. If majority of them can be answered affirmatively, chances are good that the child is emotionally healthy.

1. Is the child learning to separate from his family without undue stress and to form an attachment with at least one other adult at school?
2. Is the child learning to confirm the routines at school without undue fun?
3. Is the child able to involve himself deeply in play?
4. Is the child developing the ability to settle down and concentrate?
5. Is the child unusually withdrawn or aggressive for his age?
6. Does the child have access to the full range of his feelings, and is he learning to deal with them in an age appropriate way?

Additional aspects of mental health which are covered under the development of the social self, include, learning to care for other people, cross cultural education, and taking pleasure in meaningful work.

Properly co-ordinating these methods of teachings will surely bring out the innate potential of the child with which to develop better in the future. The effect of such well brought up child to the nation building cannot be over whipped.

Teacher-Parent Relationship
Only through a close working relationship between school and home can the child truly perform at his or her creative best. Classroom life must not be isolated from the general cultural environment. Creativity, physical

and oral responsiveness, pleasure, and success are all dependent on the child's behaviour patterns and on the understanding, loving and accepting family and teacher.

The teacher-parent relationship is very much important for the development of the child because the child's behaviour observed in school by the teacher is learned first at home, through inappropriate assistance of the parent. Truly, the behaviour of children should be the number one concern of teachers if they have to succeed in helping each child develop appropriately.

This relationship is for the benefit of the child, parent, and teacher in fulfilment of a life goal. For years, teachers do not communicate with parents unless their children were having problems or needed to be punished. This is not supposed to be so, if only we all are truly committed to educating the children to become responsible adults to contribute to the social, economic, moral, and political development of the society.

Differences in educational, social, and economic levels may cause some parents to feel insecure with the teacher or in the school situation. If this is true, the teacher must take the initiative in establishing a warm relationship with such parent. When parents are not familiar with the purpose and plans for the school activities, they may be suspicious of the total programmes. They can then, as a result, block communication between home and school activities.

Some parents have a feeling of awe with teachers, while some feel resentful towards them. Some parents also feel their failing in helping their children grow and need reassurance that the teachers can do a good job as is the belief that teachers "know all and best". In this case, a conducive, cordial bridge has to be built across in order to harmonise these attitudes. And this means teachers will have to explain to parents the goals of their school programmes. A well-organised, controlled classroom with little confusion and selected activities that will immensely contribute to the development of the children, will reassure parents of the commitment and willingness of the teachers.

Sometimes teachers may want to work co-operatively with parents, but their own feelings toward parents may hinder their success. Some teachers, equally, do resent parents and blame them for the children's difficulties and misbehaviour. Unfortunately, some even see parents as a means of fulfilling their financial goals or desires, by exploiting them through unnecessary levies. There is threat and counter-threat from both sides in different forms and manners at the detriment of the children.

To be sincere, teacher-parent relationship in our society, no matter the pretence to cover-up, has never been one of mutual love, trust and respect. They have never trusted one another in their respective dealings. This has always led to the harassment of teachers by parents over issues concerning the children, and the teachers have come up with complaints over this maltreatment and disregard. The teacher's authority in school is threatened as a result of this.

Teachers then develop this "I don't care" attitude toward the educational well being of the children, resulting in the underdevelopment of these children. The children are now left at the mercy of their premature, undirected minds that could lead them to delinquencies. Therefore, teachers and parents need to recognise these problems and make efforts at solving them, as well as, recognising one another's abilities and grow concern for what is best for the one child.

In reality, parents can be partners with teachers, learning about their children and working out plans to help them. Teachers and parents have much to learn from one another about the growth of their children. Parents can help teachers understand their children, their behaviour and feelings, because what happens to a child at school must be related to what happens at home.

An understanding rapport is a must to carry the children along, giving them two friendly worlds to work in for enhanced life. It is, therefore, advisable that parents cultivate the attitude of getting totally involved in planning, implementing plans and supporting the efforts of teachers in various ways, such as, sharing with them information on the child's interests, health or any other pertinent area.

In order to foster this teacher-parent involvement, home visit on the part of teachers is necessary. This home visit idea can be timed and scheduled with some flexibility to suit both parties in order to guarantee many more visits and make them pleasurable. It is a time they can share information about the child's progress in learning to aid each other's role. Sometimes during such visits, the teacher may notice unsanitary conditions that are hazardous to the child's health and advise the parents on what to do, he/she can even go ahead to discuss it with the proper school authority which may also act as the agent of change with the right community agency.

But when on a home visit teachers should be cautious in discussing certain issues that may cause fear, uneasiness and inferiority in parents especially those trying to cope with their seeming hopeless conditions. This will help avoid resentful reactions which can intimidate teachers and likewise discourage one more visit.

Sensitivity to the family value system, current needs, ways in which the family is meeting these needs, independence of the family and cultural influences provide means by which a teacher can interpret children's responses to their school environment. This will enable the teacher to know what not to discuss when home visit is undertaken. Home visits are developed on positive attributes of children, though teachers should recognise the negative factors to aid them in meeting parents and children's needs. This visit shouldn't be only for complaints, but also to plan the right kind of activities for the child's peculiar skill or talent.

Teachers should be taken in confidence by parents when discussing, this way, the teacher sees issues discussed as being confidential and treated as such. No gossiping, blackmailing, scandalising or slandering using the information gotten during discussion.

There are some parents who don't understand their role in their children's learning processes, it is the teacher who can educate them on this matter. The materials teachers share and the discussions they have with parents should serve as aids rather than answers in thinking through their decisions regarding their own children. General knowledge of certain patterns of growth or development should help parents accept differences of the children within their own family, as well as, differences within their age group. Teachers must recognise that parents will implement these ideas discussed about their children according to their home environments, values and morals.

Teacher-Parent Conferences
There are basically two types of teacher-parent conferences: whole/group and individual.

Individual Conference

This is the personal meeting between the teacher and the parent of each child at a convenient time for both. In this case, the parent should be encouraged to discuss the child and the family in general terms. The teacher should be the listener, the guide for the discussions with pertinent questions, and one who express for having the child in the classroom. The individual conference is based on personal need, interest, and accomplishment. This may be held in the classroom, teachers' lounge, or in the home. The teacher should jot down whatever information about the child during this meeting as a reference.

Suggestions for Individual Conference

Place
Choose a place convenient for both parent and teacher.

Time
Schedule the conference after school, at lunch or when it is convenient. Do not have too many conferences in the same day. Parents would not come when they know they will wait for too long before talking with the teachers.

Before Conference
The teacher should have the child's folder available for reference. Let the teacher inform the child about the meeting and its benefit to the child.

Opening the Conference
The parent should be made to feel at ease by keeping the setting as formal as possible. Remember the parent wants an honest report but also has fear that the child is not doing well.

During the Conference
The teacher should start with positive comment on the child before discussing any problem. Listen carefully and you will learn much that will aid you deal with the child. Concentrate on any possible solution that can help both of you work together to help the child.

Closing the Conference
Keep the conference short and end it with an optimistic note or remark.

After the Conference
Report in the child's folder the date of the meeting and a few relevant comments.

Form Diagram
Table 5.9: Form Reviewing Child's Strengths and Weaknesses With Parents

```
Child's Name: _____
Parent's Name: _____
Date: _____
Phone call_____Home visit_____School visit_____
Review of curriculum for the child _____
_____
_____
Review of the child's performance _____
_____
_____
Review of special needs_____
Review of teacher's plan for meeting child's needs_____
_____
_____
Suggestions for parent involvement_____
_____
```

Suggestions for Recording Child's Development for Individual Conference

September: Evaluate individualised skills and performances on rating form.

October-December: Make detail record on each child

January: Re-evaluate individualised skills and performances. Summarise detail records. Hold individual conference with parents.

February April: Add more detailed record to child's folder.
May: Re-evaluate individualised skills and performances. Summarise detailed records for the year. Write a report of progress. Hold individual conferences with parents.

The Whole Conference (PTA)

This conference involves long hours, therefore it should be planned well and should start as early in the school year as possible. The Parent-Teacher Association Conference can be an overview of the year's programmes; an examination of materials and children's work; an explanation of certain phrases of instruction; or can feature a guest speaker on general topics of interest like behaviour, health problems, or the teaching techniques. This is when teacher-parent involvement in planning and in how to implement these plans are discussed properly.

A wise teacher keeps parent informed with accurate point by point information concerning the behaviour and abilities of their children which have to be presented in such conference. During this conference, teachers should be able to help parents to help their children in the selection of purchase materials; give them constructive ways to involve their children in home activities which they must demonstrate to the children; help parents by making a list of various events, places, or things to do in the community, and list of appropriate books at the public library; to be creative and think up special ideas for special children. All these will help parents provide good learning environment for their children at home.

The joint efforts of teachers and parents will strengthen the children's ability to learn and provide satisfactory accomplishment of their development physically and mentally. Just as teachers commit themselves to the educational well being of parents and their children, the parents too should be interested and committed to the welfare of the teachers, because this has a direct influence on the teachers and children's performances in the classroom, vis-à-vis, the society. Teachers must be considered able to communicate properly to these parents by way of sending a monthly newsletter on classroom activities; bulletin board displayed near the school entrance where parents pick up their children; weekly folder of children's work, especially written newspaper articles.

A special booklet may be made available on general policies and school information.

Giving and receiving are basic human patterns and provide for expression of love, affection, and sharing. Thus, we show courtesy and respect for others' dignity, integrity and ability. Teachers and parents have no better way than inculcating this basic attitude of give and take among themselves in order to help the children develop in their learning process.

The detailed school curriculum with planned programmes for the children can be developed and executed by the teacher as in the example in Table 5.10.

Table 5.10: Daily Activity Schedule for 3-Year Olds

Teacher:

Date:
Major activities of the previous day: drawing around bodes; field trip to student health centre

Time	Staff	Activity	Self	Purpose
8.15-910		Teachers begin setting up	Social, emotional, physical	To be prepared for the morning
9.00-9.15		Gate/locker	Social, emotional	Children are familiar with the song. Helps them recognise body parts and use them in a creative way
9.10-9.30		Song (10 little fingers)	Emotional, physical	Children are familiar with the song. Helps them recognise body parts and use them in a creative way.
			Cognitive, physical	They have to remember the rhyme and they are using body parts (all fingers)

	Head, shoulders, knees and toes	Physical, cognitive	Ordering of the body parts they are familiar with it. Good large muscle movements during group activity
	Discuss "feeling" pictures	Emotional, social	This helps children come to terms with their feelings. They realise that others have these feelings too. It also helps them understand these feelings
	Book - if I did awful, would you still love me?		Generate feelings of acceptance. Share possible feelings of rejection
9-30-10.05 Self-select	Blocks, rubber, animals, people	Cognitive, creative	Create from the blocks uses for animals and people. Ordering and counting skills with the blocks. Build house, etc. Realise what people and animals need: same things for different ones.
	Finger: painting white, red, blue	Emotional cognitive, creative, physical	Use as a tension-relieving experience. Self-expression. Make fingerprints. Learn that only they have those fingerprints. Compare one to another. They learn how to mix the colours and how much paints and

			starch to use. I hope the colours make pastels with white. Feeling paint.
	Dramatic play with family puppets, particularly doctor and nurse puppets; hospital dresses	Creative, social, emotional, physical	They are creating situations by working out any feeling for situation from home. They are working together. they have command of the puppets and so strengthen their egos. They have to use fine muscles to manipulate the puppets
	Making snacks: peanut butter sandwiches	Cognitive, Physical, social	Being able to create snack and use a knife gives children a sense of competence. They learn ordering which goes on first. They can also help the rest of the group. Non-sexist
	Let's find out/ multicultural - already set up (comparison of ways mothers carry babies around	Social, cognitive	Teach them about things in their environment. Broaden their acceptance of people and culture different from their own. Teach children people have similar need but solve them in a variety of practical ways
	Large muscles/boxes with flashlights	Creative	They will need to be creative, deciding on various uses for the boxes

		Physical, cognitive	They will be able to crawl in and out of the boxes and be aware of the boxes touching their bodies. They become aware of their place in space
		Emotional	Deal with fear of darkness — controlling dark themselves by using flashlight
		Cognitive	They learn which boxes (smaller, larger) they can fit in, which body parts can go in first, and which came out last.
		Social	They Work together on the use of the boxes and sharing them
10.05-10.15 clean up/ toilet time	Physical, social, emotional		Transition to snack. The children enjoy feeling the soap and water, can discuss hot and cold. Learn orderliness and responsibility cleaning up. Feels good to use the toilet
10.15-10.30	Snacks peanut butter, sandwiches apple slices, juice	Physical, social, emotional	Discuss body parts; eating pineapple swallowing hard and

				soft foods and how it feels. Chance to discuss with teacher and other students. Sharing time/personalities. Nutrition. Responsibility in cleaning up afterwards.
10.30-11.30 outside activities	Use shovels		Cognitive, physical, creative	Learn cause and effect of soft and hard ground, use muscles digging the hard ground and shovelling. Create alternate ways to dig dirt and sand up
	Trikes with wagon (new ones)		Physical, social	Give others a ride. Working together using more physical strength to put two. locomotion.
	Balls - throw or kick toward fence; over and under equipment		Physical, creative	This will take eye-foot and eye-hand ordination. Creativity as to where to throw or kick it and wether to kick it high or low. Watching space and others. Projectile management.

REFERENCES

Adesina, S. 1982. "Trends and Challenges of Primary Education in Nigeria." In Adesina, S. and Ogunsaju, S. (eds.) *Primary Education in Nigeria*. Ibadan: Board Publications Ltd.

Adesina, S. 1982. *Planning and Educational Development in Nigeria*. Lagos: Board Publications.

Asiedu - Akrofi, K. 1985. *The Professional and Personal Development of the Teacher*. Lagos: Evans Brothers Ltd.

Gagne, R. 1970. *Conditions of Learning*. New York: Holt, Rinehart & Winston.

Galloway, A. 1976. *Psychology of Learning and Teaching*. New York: McGraw-Hill Book Co.

Hoyle, E. 1974. "Professionality, Professionalism and Control in Teaching". *London Educational Review* 3(2):13-19.

Lowman, J. 1987. *Mastering the Techniques of Teaching*. New York: Prentice-Hall.

Marland, M. 1975. *The Craft of the Classroom*. London: Heinemann.

Menges, R.J. 1977. *The International Teacher*. New York: Cole Publishing Co.

Nwankwo, J.I. and Nwankwo, E.I. 1984. *Principles and Practice of Teaching as a Profession*. Ibadan: Ibadan University Press.

Okorie, J.U. 1979. *Fundamentals of Teaching Practice*. Enugu: Fourth Dimension Publishing Co. Ltd.

Onwuegbu, O.I. 1979. *Discover Teaching*. Enugu: Fourth Dimension Publishing Co. Ltd.

Schmuck, R.A. and Schmuck, P.A. 1979. *Group Processes in the Classroom*. London: W.M.C. Brown Co. Publishers.

Chapter Six

SOCIAL VICES AND VIOLENCE

In this chapter, we shall discuss how important it is to start educating the child early for his or her better development, to benefit not only the child, but also the society. In the same way, we will have to grasp the negative role which abuse and neglect are playing on this desired development of the child and how they have become part of the obstacles to achieving this.

In addition to this menace is the social violence resulting from some aspects of the abuse and neglect of the child, such as, prostitution, child labour, drug addiction, ritual (cults), with all their attendant vices etc. To be examined also are some of these social ills which serve as a pointer to the extent to which child education has declined in Nigeria.

These have not only deprived the child of his or her rightful place in the society, but have equally deprived the nation and still going to strip it in future of its potential and viable labour force which will be detrimental to the nation's development if no quick intervention is made now.

What is Child Abuse?
Steele (1974) has defined child abuse as a particular type of parent-child relationship, which can exist in a combination of any other psychological state like depression, schizophrenia, psychosomatic illness, and other character disorder which still takes a psychiatric stance in his definition.

It may be added that this definition cannot be generalised for all cases of child abuse in Nigeria, where it is either seen as a bye-product of poverty or as a norm. This is so because Nigerians value their children so much that some rich parents can even spoil their children through over pampering, while the very poor can overwork, sometimes "punish" the children to make sure that they become useful to themselves and the society.

Whichever way we look at it, most cases of child abuse in Nigeria can be ascribed to poverty rather than character disorder. Since some abusers feel dependent and lonely, they don't seek help from adults, instead they take solace in their abused children.

However, an unwanted baby can resort to child abuse as the child is already hated ever before it was born. In extreme case, the child is even abandoned after birth.

Apart from the aforementioned causes of child abuse, the rest include alcoholism, drug addiction, impossible living conditions, disrespect for human life, unbearable stress, spiritual bankruptcy and distorted or misplaced values. Whatever the case, both the culprit and victim of abuse need help. Petterson and Roscor (1983) have remarked that neglect occurs not as a form of punishment but as a result of wanting to meet children's needs.

Child Abuse and Neglect

Child abuse and neglect has to be redefined from time to time. The focus on child abuse and neglect, in the context of the family unit leads to a narrowing down of definitions of child abuse and neglect. In other words, we fall into the trap of seeing individual trees without seeing the forest.

What happens to children in war zones? Families break up, leading to the separation of children from their parents, the occupation forces abuse children, especially girls who are mercilessly raped and then killed. Children who are alive are in great risk from the time of hostilities until relative peace returns to their place of origin. The general reaction to hostilities is evacuation. Three categories of children are important to distinguish at this stage — children who are already separated or orphaned, children who run away without consent of parents and children who are directed by parents to go to safer places. Those who are in the country end up in camps or feeding centres or they drift by themselves into the streets of urban areas.

With relative peace returning to the occupied areas, people gradually return to their place of origin. Children who were evacuated with knowledge of parents are likely to be reunited with them if they are still alive. This is also true for children who fled without their parents' consent. However, the homeless children will need placement. Those who were previously in orphanages may have to look for foster parents to be adopted. This process is an agonising one and children at many points along the road are subject to abuse and death.

There are five kinds of child abuse, which include physical abuse, verbal abuse, emotional abuse, emotional neglect and sexual abuse.

Physical Abuse

This is a bodily injury which the abusive parent may inflict on the child. There are wide varieties of physical injuries which includes beating pushing against an object, twisting the ear or lip, pouring cold water on the whole body, flogging, asking the child to kneel down for hours or lift up heavy object he/she is unable to lift, burning a part of the body, putting pepper into the child's eyes, making cuts on the child's body, it can go on and on.

Emotional Abuse

In emotional abuse, the parents depend on the child. The parent-child role is reversed. The child with his limited capabilities cannot meet the demands and therefore has to run away from the family environment and its hardship. Instances of this category in Nigeria can emanate from sickness or laziness on the part of parents. It can also be found in a one parent family where the existing parent lays his/her full reliance on the child for support.

In this day of mass retrenchment and unemployment of parents, one can suspect that many Nigerian children are suffering from emotional abuse which can result in poor academic performance. That some children also hawk wares before and after school session each day and are left with no time to play, relax or think for themselves is a pointer to emotional child abuse. Again the problem revolves around poverty or ignorance on the part of parents of what the child needs.

Emotional Neglect

According to Parents Anonymous Organisation Report (1978), emotional neglect can be the most demanding of all the abuses. This is where the parents show no sign of love or hatred towards the child. Thus, the child feels empty. Nigerian parents are prone to demonstrating their love for the children through actions of favour and are not given to verbal "I love you" syndrome found in the Western world. It becomes important at this time of hardship for parents to learn to explain the economic situation to the child to avoid unnecessary misinterpretation of parents' inability to provide for his/her needs.

Sexual Abuse

This has not been found very common due to the fact that all societies regard incest as taboo. When it does occur at all, it is often between mother and son. This kind of abuse is hard to deal with, since it is usually handled behind closed doors. The case of sexual abuse by adults on children is on the increase these days. Children are being raped every now and then, this has caused trauma to these children who are victims.

Verbal Abuse

Verbal abuse is the most commonly used. This includes raining insults on the child, shouting or screaming at him and telling him he is not worth a kobo. Very often, this kind of abuse becomes inseparable from emotional abuse.

Causes of Child Abuse

Causes of child abuse vary. They include cruelty, which is mistaken for a pattern of rearing. Many abusers don't know any other pattern of child rearing.

The abuser as a child may not have established the basic trust. The abuser may not have had the emphatic mothering experiences as a child, hence, as an adult the abuser mistrusts fellow adults. She was disappointed by the mother, thus, the only person she can look upon for the lost love and care is her own child. She sees the child as existing to solve her problem. Making this demand when the child is totally unprepared, lead the child to abuse.

Political Violence

Another global issue which requires more attention is political violence affecting children. In 1976 Kwezi Kadeile with 400 young demonstrators in the South African township of Soweto gave an account of his experience as reported by Amnesty International Report; the killing of 50 to 100 children between ages 8 and 16 in 1970 by the Imperial Guard as ordered by the deposed Emperor Bokassa.

These children had protested against the purchasing of government prescribed school uniforms produced by a factory owned by Bokassa. The children were bayoneted or beaten to death with sharpened sticks and whips. Others were suffocated to death. Who are these agents of political violence? Where do they draw their power from? What support do they have to perpetuate their obnoxious acts?

Abject Poverty

Let me now turn to another key issue which influences the well being of children, that is abject poverty. As shown in figure 6.1, marked structural inequalities in distribution of resources and development benefits, prevalence of disease, droughts and military rule combine to bring abject poverty and misery to the Nigerian children. Abject poverty in turn leads to several dehumanising paths for children.

The first path is the merchandising of children. This is the case of babies who are snatched away from their mothers and sold through clandestine channel. From time to time, the culprits are caught without severe punishment.

The other way of merchandising children is a straight commercial transaction. Children are obtained for sale through abduction from institutions such as maternity wards of hospitals, wherein the staff operate a "baby sales business" or even from parents themselves. The sale of children takes an international dimension, in Nigeria through "legalised" adoption (using bribes). Very little information is available on how the "children's market" operate.

The few cases reported by the newspapers are not even studied by the concerned agencies. Offenders often get punished but there is little understanding on casualty both on the agents supplying these children and the agents on the demand side. Abject poverty of families has been cited as a major cause for parents selling their children. They have to make the crucial choice between selling their children or being starved to death. But the "children's market" is a complete one.

The offering of children's labour, though socially acceptable, could lead to the exploitation of these children by their employee. Child labour is a studied area of Child Abuse.

A sample of African Countries Showing the Following Figure of Children Between 10 to 14 Years Old Forming Part of the Labour Force

Percentage
Egypt	-	11.5
Ivory Coast	-	43.0
Mali	-	45.04
Mozambique	-	28.1
Tanzania	-	29.9
Burkina Faso	-	44.0
Nigeria	-	53.0

However, a child as young as 5 years old can already be in the labour force. Generally, their working conditions are harsh and detrimental to their development. They are malnourished, lacking in recreational opportunities, unable to go to school and unable to save any money as they are only given enough for their subsistence. Frankly, they have no future.

It is, therefore, important to study these conditions of work, starting from the household unit as the user of child labour as well as the provider of child labour in society. Integration into society and individual development are processes which no longer take place within the family, and which is increasingly drained of its meaning and content. Much more, the family whose social role has been destroyed is bound to have something of a similar effect on the child who is no longer seen as a value in his own right but as a "spare wheel".

How to Stop Child Abuse and Neglect in Nigeria
As mentioned earlier, most abusers in Nigeria are poor. Child abuse and

neglect due to poverty can be separated from that of cruelty, if the economic situation of the average Nigerian improves. That is to say, poverty must be eradicated.

Organisation aimed at eradicating child abuse and neglect should be formed in Nigeria. Such organisations can start articulating the child abuse problem to educate and help the understanding of the abuser. Such organisation like the newly formed African Network for the Prevention and Protection Against Child Abuse and Neglect (ANPPCAN) and Planned Parenthood Federation of Nigeria would aim at helping the abuser as well as the abused.

The Social Welfare Office is an arm of the government and can only pursue what is articulated and guided by law. The government, therefore, should define what can be termed as child abuse in this society, and legislate it without disrupting the people's culture. The states can set up committees and draw up programmes to fight child abuse and neglect. In such programmes, parents should learn more about children's capabilities and limitations. The government must support financially, programmes that have been proven effective in eliminating child abuse.

Family planning must be encouraged among Nigerians to avoid excessive children that cannot be catered for. Pre-marriage counselling will also help. The Government should see that only those who have adequate provision of housing, feeding, education, etc, should be allowed to have an extra wife, be it Muslim, Christian or naturalist. Those parents who abuse or neglect their children's welfare should be severely punished.

Mass retrenchment and unemployment of parents should stop to ease parents' frustration which might manifest in child abuse. Schools and hospitals must co-operate in reporting cases of child abuse. Although a reported parent may feel angry at first, in the long run, he/she will be pleased that somebody intervened.

Universities and colleges of education can create courses for parents and parents-to-be on the evils of child abuse, stress and how to cope with it.

The media is indispensable in the prevention of child abuse. Therefore, the Nigerian Mass Media should take the issue of child abuse seriously.

There might be chronic child abusers who might be found among alcoholics and drug addicts. Such people should have their abused children taken away from them.

More individuals and organisations should show interest in developing programmes for the well being of the child.

Child Labour

This has been briefly mentioned earlier, but it deserves more elaboration here. There have been problems as to the cultural and legal definitions of a child. The first problem, which is cultural, relates to whether persons of the ages of 12-16 years who are married should no longer be regarded as children. Among the Hausas of Northern Nigeria, females of about 10-12 years, when betrothed, are admitted into womanhood. And since they have unofficially assumed adult roles, tasks performed by them are regarded as work, therefore are taken to be child labour.

The second problem concerns the legal definition. Whereas the children Law of 1958 defines a child as "any person who has not yet attained the age of 14 years", the Nigerian Labour Decree of 1974 is not precise over this, where section 58(1) considers a child as any person below 15 years of age, section 58(3) and (8) set the ages of 14 and 16 respectively. Not withstanding these differences, a child is regarded as any person below the age of 18 years.

What is child labour? It could be defined also as any physical or mental exertion of body undertaken wholly or in part by any person below the age of 18 years with a view of some reward, which would be in kind, or cash, for the person or any other person. Child labour can be seen as an exploitation of the child for gain. Exploitation as interpreted by the children and young persons in law as "making unreasonable or excessive use of the services of a child or young persons for monetary profit". Another interpretation by Marxists of exploitation is "appropriation of surplus value or labour, by a person other than the direct producer, either in the process of production or in the process of circulation.

Child labour occurs in two contexts: family and society context. In the family, children are engaged in domestic work, farm and errands. Outside the family (society), children are made to perform economic activities such as newspaper vending, bus conducting, shop operating, street trading, public entertainment and employment in textile industry, hotels and restaurants.

A conceptual view of child labour tends to see it as a form of socialisation whereby children are groomed to become thrifty and industrious. This concept is in line with the philosophy of the puritans and the Quakers (Friedlander, 1976). According to Schildrout, 1980, child labour is a form of mutual dependence between adults and children. This means the whole family structure is made up of parts, with each part having its functions to play and being mutually dependent on one another.

These views are wrong because they trample on the rights of the child and destroy his or her development towards living a meaningful life; this is exploitation of children, premature assumption of adult roles, working long hours for low wages, damage of their physical and psycho-social health and denial of the opportunities for their education and recreation.

The problem of child labour obviously does not feature as a part of a socialisation or phenomenon which may facilitate growth and development, but the negative aspect which hinders the educational development of the child. Thus, children are compelled to join the work force in their early years for their own and families' survival, which has led to exploitation and deprivation.

This phenomenon of child labour is seen more in developing countries like Nigeria where it is more pronounced in urban areas than in rural areas, though this is beginning to change now as children in the rural areas are engaging more and more in economic activities for survival.

Street Hawking

Street hawking has been an aspect of child labour practice in Nigeria for more than a century. It is also seen as an aspect of child abuse which is next to emotional abuse because it subjects the child to long hours of child labour — starvation and deprivation of adequate care. Historically and traditionally, Nigerians place very high value on children, but in spite of this, children are treated by some parents as commodity.

Some parents give out their children to serve strangers for monetary gain. The child-rearing pattern of Nigerians until very recently, was based on the philosophy of children being seen and not heard.

The battering of a child or starving of a child, or child-labour for long period of time, were considered as normal way of rearing children in order to make children useful to themselves. Traditionally, the Nigerian belief is that children are God-sent helpers for economic reasons and for other purposes; this view is held by most parents.

Many parents manhandle their children because of their own life experiences, such that, most parental disciplinary practices are the result of their socialisation processes. This suggests that most of the parents whose children are participating in street hawking may have themselves been street hawkers sometime in the past. The use of their children as hawkers may largely neglect their value orientation.

Causes of Child Labour
Children have always worked. In the best circumstances, children's work prepares them for productive adult life. But then, a balance of children's work, learning and play has to be maintained. Such balance, unfortunately, is not always maintained resulting in the incidence of child labour. Some of the causes of this can be classified as stated thus:

1. Tradition and Culture
In most parts of Nigeria, parents see the birth of children as a means of adding to the household labour force. For this reason, they are motivated to having many children who will carry out various family work. Children are then trained early to rehearse adult roles by taking part in their parent's social and economic activities. Some of these activities are opportunities to act out behaviour required of them in future as adults.

During this process of socialisation, the child grows in physical and intellectual maturity without ill treatment and virtually without being exploited — the work is practically free from harmful effects. In the northern parts of Nigeria, the Hausa-Fulani cattle rearers are examples as well as the Ibo yam farmers. Very many of the children consider it quite normal that they should not attend school but continue the family tradition of working at an early age.

Early marriage is another aspect of culture which initiates young children into adulthood and impose on them adult roles. They have to work to survive with their new families' responsibilities.

2. Poverty
The traditional belief of having many children for economic reasons in the past is having adverse effect on most families in present modern time. The decline of mortality rate of children has resulted in survival of large number of children.

Unfortunately, with the backwardness in economic development, combined with poor management of national resources and an undemocratic political setting (military adventurism), many families are plagued by poverty. These poor families with more children are heavily dependent on their young children to survive, since they cannot afford to employ persons in the prescribed working age. Thus, perpetuating child labour among them.

3. Poor Scholastic Achievement
A child playing the dual role of working to help the family survive (economic role) and going to school to acquire formal education (academic role) is bound to confront "role strain". Such strain is likely to cause reduction in performance of either of the two roles; the lack of financial support from the parents and in the struggle to meet these financial needs, the child preferably will reduce in his or her academic performances. Eventually, the child drops out of school for doing badly in school studies, and feels he or she does not fit in.

4. Home Condition
The situation at home may provoke tension and uncertainty; the father may abandon the family, the mother or father may be ill, or become physically unfit or die. The disappearance of the family breadwinner may indeed force a young child to take up a job in order to financially support the family for survival.

The contributions of the psychological, social, cultural, economic and political factors in the prevalence of child labour are interlinked, thus the impact of one factor can be studied only in relation to the other. Thus, any examination of these factors of child labour should consider their interaction in any given state.

Effects of Child Labour on the Child

Health Problem
The health of exploited working children is being endangered by allowing them to work under hazardous health conditions. These working children come from poorer segments of the population. Thus, they start from the

disadvantaged health status as they suffer malnutrition due to poor feeding habit. Their work raises their nutritional requirements, which they are mostly unable to meet and become vulnerable to diseases.

Malnutrition
Normal child growth which spurts puberty and adolescence, are adversely affected by the poor nutrient intake and increased manual work. Studies have shown that malnutrition in early childhood continuing into adolescence adversely affects their body weight. This also affects the physical, mental and social development of the child.

Occupational Hazards
Children, in work situation, come in close contact with infectious diseases as their immune system is broken down by severe malnutrition, anaemia, hard labour, fatigue and inadequate sleep or rest. These children are mostly given dirty jobs which adults will not easily do, e.g. trash collection from garbage spots through which they are exposed to unsanitary conditions of living. At work some are exposed to toxic substances which they may inhale or have body contact with.

For instance, the effects of lead poisoning for brocade manufacturing workers who inhale very fine particles of Zari have been documented. Injuries are immediate. Many diseases which can take decades to manifest, for example, asbestosis, chronic cadmium toxicity and cancer, may be the result of early exposure to occupational hazards.

Psycho-social Hazards
Childhood is the stage for personality formation. The physical and emotional stress of work combined with the denial of opportunities to play, explore the world, interact fully with peers, physical and emotional abuse and neglect, separation from family, monotony and the burdens of premature responsibility is likely to have permanent adverse psychological impact. The children suffer frustration, role-conflicts and lack educational aspirations.

Educational Status, Access and Utilisation
Child labour causes children to lack in educational aspirations which have led to having majority of them being illiterate or semi-illiterate. Only few

of the working children attend school, fewer can combine earning and learning which is very difficult because of the long hours of working. Some are "dropouts" and since certifications from schools, colleges and universities give better employment opportunities, such educational deprivation bars these children from any chances of better employment in life.

In some cases, instead of schooling, children are given out as apprentices. This practice itself has become a severe form of exploitation of children. Children are put to apprenticeship for years to avoid wages and other facilities, or used as servants to do the tasks unrelated to the skills of the trade.

The effects of children working at an early age cannot be overlooked, because it destroys the child and leads to social violence, the result of degeneration of mental development.

It is possible that when a child begins to work and especially when he or she leaves the family circle to engage in such a job, there are bound to be problems. This stage of development is the period of profound mental change in the child. If the negative intellectual development is allowed to combine with his or her ill-directed mental development, as is always the case today, there are bound to be undesirable consequence and behaviour problems.

Many of these children take to dangerous habits, such as drinking alcohol (beer and local gin), drug and sexual abuse, armed robbery etc. These arise from the fact that he or she now assumes himself or herself to be an adult, thus imitating, distorting and exaggerating what he or she wrongly believes to be the essence of that world. These failings, with his or her lack of adequate general education and vocational training, will restrict his or her ability to make a significant contribution to the society. A damaging degree of cognitive impoverishment may occur as a result of lack of adequate facility for mental growth.

It turns out that when the children realise that they are being cheated and deprived; the feeling of injustice and frustration from being unable to achieve what others have done in living a comfortable life, can cause permanent negative effect on personal relationships and even lead to aberrations of behaviour and personality. Social hostility sets in. The physical development is not spared.

Research reports (Desoille 1976) in Japan indicated that children who start work before the age of 14 years were found to be on the average, 4cm short than those who entered after 18 years old. Heavy loads and awkward positions can affect physical growth of the bones. The malnutrition of these children can endanger their central nervous system.

Child labour will continue to be avenue for social violence in the society if nothing is quickly done to eliminate this inhuman act on the cognitive development of the child. The nation shall equally continue to be at a loss as to the required viable manpower for its economic development in the future.

Drug Abuse

A visit to centres for the cure of drug addiction will show that drug abuse cases are on the increase. No person is born an addict, rather, it is a product of the interaction between environment and social factors.

One may ask, "what is a drug"? Simply put, it is any substance which when taken into the body could modify one or more of the body functions. Drug dependence, which may be physical or psychic (emotional), is a continuous desire to take drug to produce pleasure or to avoid discomfort. It is usually self-administered with the primary action on the central nervous system in a manner that deviates from the approved medical or social pattern.

Drug abuse which has invaded schools, colleges and universities, and the society at large, stemmed from educational neglect and deprivation of the children. A study (Yoloye, 1991) indicated that 9.2% of the adolescents in Nigeria were self-confessed drug dependent. Most of the so-called "dropout" or "misfit" children are being used for drug trafficking in their desire to attain financial independence. Obviously, this led them to addiction.

This issue of drug abuse is of paramount importance in recent times because most crimes like armed robbery, assassination, vandalism, theft, among others, are often committed while under the strong influence of hard drugs such as indian hemp, cocaine, heroine, etc. The addicts will go to any extent to procure the drug to satisfy his/her desire, thereby involving in theft and other social vices to get the money for it.

The dependence on drug, which leads to abuse, destroys the physical and mental conditions of those who engage in it. They suffer from cirrhosis of the liver, brain damage, etc. and as such, become not just a burden to themselves, but also a burden to the society. Instead of contributing meaningfully to the development and integration of the society, these individuals rather constitute social and economic problem. Umoh (1991) aptly sums the importance of this problem thus:

> In view of the negative consequence which drug abuse brings to drug abusers, it is necessary to enlighten the youths, as well as the adults on what drug abuse is, its causes and its effects. This is important because the youths are the leaders of tomorrow and it will be a tragedy to handover the mantle of leadership to drug abusers.

Causes of Drug Abuse
Some of the environmental factors which can cause drug abuse include:
1. Self-help activities
2. Poor home condition (lack of parental care and protection)
3. Peer group influence
4. Occupational stress
5. Lack of employment (idleness)

For some social reasons, drug abusers want to:
1. Achieve a sense of belonging; the desire to be accepted by others
2. Express independence of thought and action, and to alleviate fear
3. Have a pleasurable, new, thrilling or dangerous experience
4. Gain an improved understanding of creativity of extra energy (endurance)
5. Foster a sense of relation and sedation

All these lead to the psychological need to escape from reality because of the lack of strength, courage and willingness to confront the problems of everyday life. This may raise the desire to rebel against the society and its harsh rules.

Types of Drugs
1. Marijuana (Indian hemp)
2. Cocaine
3. Heroine
4. LSD
5. Librium
6. Valium
7. Sleepless tablets
8. Proplus
9. Reactivan
10. Dexamphetamine

Indian hemp (Marijuana) ranks the highest among the abused drugs by youths.

Solution
Despite all the efforts put in by the government in establishing some centres for the curing of drug addiction, and the vigorous public enlightenment mounted by both the government and non-governmental organisations, the abuse of drug has continued to increase. Are these adequate solutions to drug abuse? If they are, why have they not helped in reducing drug abuse among young children? If not, then something that needs to be done to eliminate it has not been done. As it is commonly said, "prevention is better than cure". This remains true even in this case.

The problem of drug abuse is more psychological (mental orientation) than any thing else. Pursuing the effects of drug abuse rather than the causes is a waste of time, energy and resources. To minimise, if not completely eliminate drug abuse among the young children, there must be a revisit to the basics - early childhood education - with all intent and purpose. The manner in which a child is mentally prepared in his or her early age, tells on the physical and social development of that child.

A total commitment to early childhood education will be laying a solid foundation for children's mental and physical development to become adults with commitment to social and economic responsibilities.

Back to the basics, in addition to what has been discussed earlier on early childhood education, is improving and effectively implementing early child education programmes to give the right mental orientation that will instil confidence and self-identity to the child, so that he or she need not resort to drug to alleviate fear and depression. Frustration is out of the way because they can fit in any occasion without feeling out of place. This means an early mental development through a comprehensive educational programmes will provide the elusive solution to drug abuse among children.

That is to say, effort has to be geared towards this, for if children study or learn according to a predetermined schedule, the tendency to use drugs for study may be minimised and gradually eliminated. The role of the school is to help build in each child, a positive self-concept and high self-esteem in himself or herself. This is a panacea for children's drug abuse, which is a threatening social problem today.

Cult
"A system of religious worship, especially one that is expressed in rituals"
The above definition, taken from the *Oxford Advanced Learner's Dictionary* supports the fact that there is nothing wrong being devoted to the practice of one's belief and worship, but it is negative to use this practice to bring about harm, destruction, death, or any form of terrorism to life and property of the next person.

In schools, colleges and universities, the deadly act of cult members is one of serious concern to all. The society is not at all exempted, for this is where cult practices are groomed. When critically looked into, they portray the negative nature of the society, therefore, it is a social problem.

The destructive practice of these cult members, who are mostly children, has gone to the extent of ritual killings, assassinations, armed robbery, sexual abuse, kidnapping, among other atrocities being committed. Lives are being seriously threatened, educational system is being disrupted in colleges and universities, and life has become a nightmare in institutions of higher learning even the society as a whole.

The fact about this is that these children are mainly imitating by acting out what the society is made up of. What then is the society made up of? It is simply made up of children and adults who had been deprived and denied of sound early childhood education, and as such have developed negative behavioural traits.

Their status of being termed "misfits", "dropouts" and "never-do-wells" or "good-for-nothing" have psychologically frustrated them, such that, they seek refuge cult activities. In so doing, they are trying to "belong" and build self-confidence, self-identify, self-esteem and so on, though in negative ways, that which they have failed to acquire through effective programmes for child education in their early age.

Even those children who are fortunate to be in schools, colleges or universities, are not adequately developed mentally and physically as a result of the ineffective teaching methods of these developmental programmes that do not create room to identify the child's talent, which could be skilfully developed for his or her future role as an adult.

These children are frustrated with the feeling of being out-of-place in the normal academic programmes which have not taken care of their different talents, and they develop behaviour disorders, becoming "rebels"; drug abuse becomes the new order, the only opium they need to carry on.

The terrorist acts of these cult members shall continue unabated unless mental development of each child is stressed from the early age of the child. This stabilises the emotional self for controlled behavioural pattern.

Social violence is an illness of the society that needs cure by the society and government. The proper educational development of the child matches the development of the nation.

Prostitution

This is an act of commercialising sex for economic gain. This has been on the increase in recent times involving female children of about 13 to 18 years. Many of them are dropouts from school and some are without any formal education. These children are being exposed to dangerous health problems as a result of this unholy activity in which they are engaged. In an interview conducted involving 20 prostitutes all less than 18 years of age, some of the reasons given as to why they are into it are as follows:

1. Financial Problems

The poor financial condition of some parents has left such parents unable to handle their family responsibilities. The children are then left with the responsibility of fending for themselves in order to survive. The girls among them are easily lured into prostitution and now take the position of breadwinners in their families.

2. Peer Group Pressure

Some children prostitutes are being influenced by their friends who tell them or convince them of the fun and financial benefit that go with it. To them it is a delightful social adventure. These friends go to the extent of providing all necessary help for their new "converts". These new converts may be encouraged to get "charms" to attract customers and also the use of crude "contraceptives" which may endanger their lives.

3. Conflict with Parents

The conflict between parents and child usually arises through a broken home or a generation conflict where traditional and modern life styles are believed to clash. This always leads to the child running away from home into the streets where the struggle for survival begins mostly through prostitution.

Prostitution which attracts "sugar daddies", regular and irregular customers has leashed out social violence in scenes of broken homes, street fighting, etc.

The Effects of Prostitution

The damages that prostitution has caused in our society cannot be over flogged. The scope of its effects covers the educational, social, economical and political aspects of the nation. It is a national problem that has plunged the nation into the depth of corruption. Many corrupt practices are linked to prostitution as it acts as a catalyst for the continued survival of these practices.

The female child who drops out of school or did not even attend any school because of one environmental or social reason or the other, decides to go outside the family circle to look for means of survival, she is lured into prostitution and finds out she can fulfil a lofty dream she has, if only she plays the game fully. She, therefore, spreads her tentacles which touch every part of our life as a nation bringing about dreadful effects in the following ways:

1. Economic and Political Effects

Because of their vicious desire to live an affluent life, these prostitutes go all out to influence with their feminine power (body), men placed in high positions to get contracts, better jobs which they are not qualified for and may even forge certificates.

The economic consequences of this self-indulgence are far reaching. Overestimated contracts being awarded to them are never executed, if ever done, it is either partly, which results to abandoned projects or below standard, with a short duration of usefulness that will require more funds for maintenance in the near future. Those in power conspire with their executive prostitutes to perpetrate this kind of corrupt practice that leads to mismanagement, misappropriation and embezzlement of government funds.

At the end of the day, we find out that more money is being spent on the same projects baptised with new names and the same vicious circle of contracts is maintained. Over the years such corrupt adventure has caused underdevelopment of the nation's economy.

Nothing is ever done right for the benefit of the society as a whole, always for the pursuit of self-interest. The masses then suffer under the weight of this behavioural decay. Poverty, consequently, becomes the national anthem. Most of the time, some human rights violation stems from these prostitutes who have become powerfully connected in the corridors of power, so that they use their connections to deal with their perceived foes without investigation.

Sometimes, because they are not knowledgeable about the requirements of these contracts, they often sell them to contractors who would not be committed to the satisfactory execution and completion of such contracts. Some male contractors, in their determination to be awarded contracts, use these prostitutes to sail through by offering them to the "oga" in charge. These prostitutes in their bid to get better employment, in some cases, will sell their bodies to get employed though not qualified. Certificates are often forged to meet the required qualification.

This has often led to drop in the employees' performance due to the inefficiency of the unqualified employee who could not carry out her duty properly. Most of the time there is no sanction or punishment for this inefficient employee because of such sexual relationship between the female employee (a prostitute) and the male employer. In the long run, such company collapses. The frequent occurrence of company collapse does not help the economy to grow.

2. Social and Education Effects

More children are lured into prostitution by those who are already practising it. They convince their converts by way of exhibiting what seem to be their financial benefits. School children are being used by these professional prostitutes to gain favour from men in high places, thereby introducing these young ones very early into the trade. Many of such children do abandon school at last. Those who remain in school do not study any more, and to pass their exams, they have to use either their bodies or money gotten from prostitution to buy grades from their teachers.

This is not only happening in the primary schools, but right through secondary schools to the higher institutions of learning. Incidence of examination malpractices has been on the rise because of the indulgence of our youths in this social vice called prostitution. The crave for material acquisition among our youths has caused a decline in their willingness to study. Because many of them got admission into institutions of higher learning through this fraudulent act, the art of prostitution continues in these campuses with its attendant adverse effects on academic standard. Lecturers and professors are bought over for good grades. Graduation is not based on academic performance but on social connections. These same one-tenth baked graduates flood the labour market and are the first to get better jobs. The professional prostitutes obviously started as young children and went on to graduate in the act as matured prostitutes. Some of them who are not able to climb up the financial ladder stay at the bottom to commit all sorts of social crime.

Gender Violence

Violence against girls and women, the most pervasive violation of human rights, is deeply embedded in the Nigerian cultures, such that, many women and girls die in the process. This violence comes in many forms over the years, such as early marriage at teen ages, girls trafficking for prostitution, and female genital mutilation.

As a result, they are deprived and denied of their basic rights to nutrition, health care, education equality and often survival itself. They usually have less schooling, have more dependants on them, and also subordinates to their partners especially in the case of teen marriage.

Girls trafficking for prostitution has been on the increase recently in Nigeria. Nigerians, who act as agents, export these girls to other countries and subject them to "slave-like" prostitution in one form or the other. The aftermath of this has always been either health risk in contracting the dreaded HIV/AIDS or drug trafficking and addiction. These girls on maturation and liberation also become agents in girls trafficking. The dehumanising activity goes on without end.

For those teens who married so early, both mothers and children are faced with high risk of death. Every year 585,000 women, many of who are only in their teens die, and millions of others suffer disability and life long injuries or diseases from causes related to early pregnancy and childbirth the world over.

It is sad that nearly 99% of these death and injuries are in developing countries, with a woman in Sub-Saharan Africa facing a risk of death related to maternal causes 250 times greater than that of a woman in Western Europe. This is as reported by UNICEF.

Nigeria has a fair share of this estimate because of the practise of early girl-child marriage, mostly in the Northern part of the country, which has exposed the teen mothers to a disease called Vesico Virginal Fistula (VVF).

Another form of violence against girls is the female genital mutilation, which is usually performed as traditional rite of passage. It exposes girls to potentially fatal infections, lifelong health hazards, and psychological trauma. An estimated 2 million girls each year in at least 28 countries undergo female genital mutilation (FGM). And Nigeria is not left out in this painful ordeal. It is being practised all over the country.

The continuance of our women and girls in facing these types of violence amount to denial of their rights and advancement. Denial of the right to education traps children in a subsistence-level existence that is perpetuated from generation to generation.

Education and Advancement of Girls/Women as Against Gender Violence

Women's status is closely linked to economic, political, and social factors and is an indication of the level of civilisation of the society in their lives. Although the Universal Declaration of Human Rights and the Declaration of the Rights of the Child proclaim that every human being, a child in particular, has the right to education, this equality does not exist in the area of boys and girls education.

In 1976-68 enrolment totalled 428 million pupils, fewer girls benefited from this increase than boys; only 186 billion in that academic year in Nigeria.

A more recent information published by UNICEF on education of children in various countries, reveals that Nigeria, in 1993-1997, has a primary school enrolment ratio of 60 for boys and 58 for girls, and from 1990 - 1995, a secondary school enrolment ratio of 33 for boys as against 28 for girls. This means that more girls are less privileged to be educated than the boys.

This trend is not only impeding the personal fulfilment of women as human beings, but as well slows down the progress of the society as a whole.

Women have a meaningful contribution to make in the development and growth of Nigeria. The way to a more rational utilisation of woman power is obviously through equal education. As an accepted principle now, there have been series of international convention agreements, to project, provide and promote opportunities to achieve this equality for the interest and well being of girls and women.

Such international convention agreements as the Convention on the Elimination of All Forms of Discrimination Against Women; The World Congress Against Commercial Sexual Exploitation of Children, held in Stockholm in 1996, adopted a declaration and agenda for action to end the sexual exploitation of children. Also, the Platform for Action of the Fourth World Conference on Women (1995) calls for the elimination of violence against girls in all forms.

Through national legislation in many countries, female genital mutilation (FGM) has been legally made a criminal offence and punishable.

Nigeria, as a member of these international organisations, should pass legislation on the protection of the rights of the child and against the exploitation of girls and women for the purpose of prostitution in and outside Nigeria (human trafficking). A practical campaign at federal, state and local government levels should be vigorously embarked upon involving security agents and the public. Stiff penalties should be meted out against offenders of these laws to discourage these activities.

Most importantly, we should provide for the children's sound educational programmes, that will absorb them and keep away their attention from the enticement of these social vices.

Examination Malpractices

This is an educational vice which has turned to a social vice because it is a spill over from the decayed condition of the society into our educational system at all levels and back to the society. This is simply the act of cheating in an examination, whether internal or external, and points to the behaviour disorder of the children-juvenile delinquency.

Examination malpractice has soiled success and a mockery made of the idea of using examination as a test of knowledge or academic ability. Because examination has continued to be a way of testing the academic knowledge of student/pupils, students are more than ever determined to pass it at all cost, by hook or crook. This will persist for a long time unless our system of testing the children's abilities is modified and effected.

The role of adults in collaborating with these children to perpetuate these ills is a proof of the decayed condition of the society. It is so bad that if a child fails in an examination, he/she goes all the way to forge certificate, because there are always adults to help them achieve this.

If only discipline is instilled in our educational system and stiffer penalty is meted out against offenders, this practice is sure to be ameliorated. The present penalties of withholding, cancelling or handing over the student culprit to the police only to be released sooner when money changed hands, is not enough to deter children. Both the adult and the children involved should be fished out and severely punished.

REFERENCES

Aronson, E. and Helmreich, R. 1973. *Social Psychology.* New York: Van Nostrand Reinhold Co.

Backman, C.W. and Secord, P.F. 1968. *A Social Psychological View of Education.* New York: Harcourt Brace Jovanovich.

Bidwell, C.E. "The Social Psychology of Teaching." In R.M.W Travers (ed.) *Second Handbook of Research in Teaching.* Chicago: Rand McNally & Co.

Dubey, D.L., Edem, D.A. and Thakur, A.S. 1971. *The Sociology of Nigeria Education.* London: George Allen and Unwin Ltd..

Dubey, D.L. 1979. *The Sociology of Nigerian Education.* Lagos: Macmillan Publishers.

Epstein, C. 1968. *Intergroup Relations for the Classroom Teacher.* Boston: Houghton Mifflin Co.

Fafunwa, A.B. 1974. *History of Education in Nigeria.* London: George Allen and Unwin Ltd.

Gergen, K.J. 1969. *The Psychology of Behaviour Exchange.* Reading, Massachussetts: Addison-Wesley Publishing Co. Inc.

Sieber, S.D. and Wilder, D.E. 1973. *The School in Society: Studies in the Sociology of Education.* New York: The Free Press.

Ukaeje, B.O. 1984. *Foundations of Education.* Benin: Ethiope Publishing Corporation.

White, W.F. 1969. *Psychosocial Principles Applied to Classroom Teaching.* New York: McGraw-Hill Book Co.

Chapter Seven

PHILOSOPHY AND POLICY FORMULATION

Determining Philosophy

An education philosophy is a statement about the experiences of teaching and learning, and the choices educators make to control these experiences. Education philosophy includes: beliefs about children's growth and development and how to guide them; the broad goals of what children should be taught; and how the programme should be planned and administered. This includes, staffing, housing and equipment, scheduling, providing nutrition and health services, working with parents, assessing, recording, reporting children's progress, financing and budgeting.

An identifiable philosophy is the key to any successful early educating programme. Once a philosophy has been developed or selected, specific programme goals and objectives must be written in keeping with that philosophy. After a philosophy and goals are determined, policies must be established. In the case of Nigeria, the Federal Government is responsible for determining the guidelines for the programme's philosophy.

The following questions are examples of the types of decisions that should be consistent within a philosophy:

1. What are the goals and objectives of your early education programme — to provide an environment conducive for the development of the whole child? To teach young children academic skills? To provide

intensive instruction in areas of academic deficits and thinking skills? To develop creativity? To build a healthy self-concept? To spur self-direction in learning?

2. What provisions for children's individual differences are consistent with your programme's philosophy — should children develop at their own rates? Should you expect the same or varying levels of achievement? Are individual differences accepted in some or all of academic areas? Are individual differences accepted in some or all developmental areas (psychomotor, effective, cognitive)? Are activities child-chosen and appropriate to his own interest and developmental level or staff-tailored to meet individual differences? Are activities presented for one or several learning styles?

3. What grouping strategy is in accord with your programmes rationale- homogenous (chronological age, mental age, achievement, interest) or heterogeneous groups? Fixed or flexible? Child determined or child-interest? Large or small?

4. What staff roles are necessary to implement the learning environment as set forth in the philosophy of your programme — persons who dispense knowledge, resource persons, or persons who prepare the environment? Persons who use positive or negative reinforcement? Group leaders or individual counsellors? Academic intent specialists or social engineers? Persons who work almost exclusively with young children or who provide parent education?

5. What staff positions (director, care-givers, teachers, aides, volunteers) are needed to execute your programme? What academic or experimental qualifications are required or desired? What type of orientation or in-service training is needed? What child-staff ratio is required?

6. What equipment and materials are required — items and materials that are self-correcting or that encourage creativity? Equipment and materials designed to stress one concept or many concept? Which

require substantial or minimal adult guidance? Are they designed for group or individual use? Do they provide for concrete experiences or abstract thinking?

7. What physical arrangement is compatible with the educational philosophy and goals of your programme — differentiated or non-differentiated areas of specific activities? Fixed or flexible areas? Outside areas used primarily for learning or for success? Equipment and materials arranged for self-service by the child or for teacher distribution.

8. What schedule format is needed to facilitate your programme's philosophy and objectives — a full or half-day schedule? Same session length for all children or length of session tailored to each child's and/or parent's needs? A predetermined or flexible daily schedule based on children's interests?

9. What evaluation procedures and instruments are consistent with your programme's philosophy — evaluation of staff planning, care giving or teaching performance? Of physical arrangement, utilisation of space, equipment and materials? Continuous or specific times for evaluation? Locally developed or standardized evaluation instruments.

Many of these choices are not either/or decisions, but involve alternative choices or combinations consistent with the chosen philosophy.

Four Basic Philosophies Stemming from Developmental Theories

1. *Cognitive-interactionist*
This model focuses on the theory that a child is an active learner who adapts to his or her environment.

2. *Affective-interactionist*
This is based on the theory of psycho-social development that encompasses the learning of basic attitudes and ways of interacting with others. It emphasises the child's matching a skill to a learning task.

3. ***Behaviourist-theoretical***
This stresses the nature of the learning process as observable, measurable change in behaviour directly transmitted through teaching. The child operates on his environment in response to cues and discriminative stimuli. The role of the teacher is to prescribe objectives and tasks, use direct teaching, and selectively reinforce specific behaviour.

4. ***Developmental-maturationist***
This philosophical theory viewed learning process as best aided by a rich, non-oppressive, environment supportive of natural development.

These philosophies can be combined to come up with a comprehensive philosophy an educational developmental programme will be based on.

Establishing Policies
Determining philosophy and goals are the first step to establishing effective policies to implementing the programme.

Policies are statements of preferred means for achieving set goals and objectives. They facilitate the implementation of goals and objectives, a sort of authoritative action. The terms "rule", "regulation", "procedures" describe a specific course of action based on these policies.

The ministry or board of education is responsible for the formulation of policies on education and the programme director is responsible for the execution of these policies in a manner that will yield results. The programme director should be able to communicate to the board the need for additional programmes, changes in the existing policies of inconsistencies and also the attitudes and values of the society whenever necessary. Likewise, the methods of executing policies must be communicated well to the programme director.

Reasons for Policy
There are some reasons why it is very necessary to formulate a policy on education:

1. A policy provides basis for evaluating existing plans and for determining the merit of proposed plans.

2. A policy provides guidelines for achieving the goals of the programmes. If there is no policy or if the existing one is inadequate, there will be inconsistency in making decisions on how to achieve the goals; programmes may not be implemented satisfactorily to provide desired result and running from emergency provision of programme results in inconsistency.

3. If a policy is constant and applies equally to all (public or private), it assures fair treatment, thus, protects the programme, children, parents and staff.

4. A policy sets standard that must be adhered to, to bring about a uniform educational development.

Characteristics of Result-oriented Policies

Developing result-oriented policies requires the government (Ministry of Education) to examine its potential reliability in facilitating achievement of educational goals, avoid the frequently prevailing tradition of operating a programme by expediency, understand the technique of policy making, and devote the time required for planning and evaluating policy.

A policy is said to be viable if it has the following characteristics:

1. Policies should be developed for the various aspects of the educational programme with internal consistency that is non-contradictory.

2. All involved in the implementation of these policies must be able to interpret them clearly to maintain greater consistency. Therefore, policies must be written to avert sudden changes and be readily available for those concerned.

3. Policies should be relatively constant and followed consistently. This means that they should not change with any change in government or board membership.

4. Policies should be guidelines for establishing administrative

considerations and actions, and so should not be highly specific but allow school administrators the discretion in solving some day-to-day problems.

5. Viable policies should be dynamic — ever changing with time. Because of the necessity of having firm and current policies, a procedure may be written, or certain policies may be reviewed after a certain period of time from the effective date.

Categories of Policies
Some of the basic categories policies must cover are stated below:

1. *Administrative Policy*
   This includes the "make-up" of the school board and procedures for selecting or electing board members, the appointment and functions of the director and supervisory personnel, administrative operations such as, the "chain of command", membership and functions of various administrative councils and committees.

2. *Staff/Personnel Policy*
   This covers recruitment, selection, appointment, qualifications, job assignment, tenure, evaluation, salary schedules and fringe benefits, absences and leaves, personal and professional activities, and training.

3. *Child-Personnel Policy*
   This comprises of admission, attendance, programme services, termination of programme services, assessing and reporting children's progress, provisions for child welfare (e.g. accidents and insurance); and special activities (e.g. filed trips and class celebrations).

4. *Business Policy*
   This includes sources of funding, nature of budget, categories of expenditures, guidelines and procedures for purchasing goods and services, a system of accounts and auditing procedures.

5. *Public Relations Policy*
   This relates to participation by the public, communication with the public and other associations.

6. *Parents Policy*
   This involves ways of meeting parents' needs for participation and education, staff involvement with parents, basic procedures for parents to follow in making children's admission, withdrawal, obtaining progress reports, participation in the programme, parents' suggestions or complaints.

7. *Record Policy*
   This is the types of records to be kept, places where records are kept, which officer will be responsible for record keeping.

Nature of Planning and Administering Early Child Education Programmes

Considering the importance of the child's early years and the need to develop the child, early child education programmes ought to be planned adequately and effectively administered to actualise result in the development of the child.

These programmes must meet the needs of our diversified population and must be consistent with the educational philosophy chosen. This means the environment provided and the services rendered, are in keeping with the goals of the programmes and stimulating too.

The first step in planning these educational development programmes, is to develop a philosophical foundation and incorporate its goals into the school curriculum at various levels. All other aspects of planning, based on this philosophy, should be considered simultaneously, because all of them work and influence one another in administering programmes.

The process of planning requires some steps to be considered which are:
a. Identifying legitimate goals for the programmes.
b. Communicating these goals to those who will plan and administer these programmes.

c. Determining the process or method by which these goals will be attained.
d. Operationalising the means for their achievement, and
e. Providing for feedback and evaluation.

When all these steps are properly co-ordinated, the realisation of the goals is made possible.

Some of Our Educational Problems

National Policy on Education
The National Policy on Education has undergone changes, modifications and amendments over the years and, indeed, will continue in this sense in the future because it has to be dynamic to be able to embrace the advancement of education in Nigeria in relation to the modern world. Our new National Policy on Education since 1980 has been a laudable one that offers a bright future for the child, both for educational purposes and for social stability. It has spelt out activities and programmes for the total development of the child for future role as adult in the society.

To be informed, the policy prescribed the following curriculum activities for the primary schools:

> The inculcation of literacy and numeracy, the study of science, the study of social norms, and values of the local community and of the country as a whole, through civics and social studies; the giving of health and physical education, the encouragement of anaesthetic, creative and musical activities, the teaching of local crafts and domestic science and agriculture.

It also categorically emphasised that the degree of knowledge acquired by the children, must be manifested through **visible indications** by way of productive creativity in visible and tangible forms.

The objectives of these activities are:
1. Character and moral training and the development of sound attitude.
2. The inculcation of permanent literacy and numeracy, and the ability to communicate effectively.

3. Developing in the child the ability to adapt to his or her changing environment.

4. Providing basic tools for further educational advancement including preparation for trades and crafts of the locality.

5. The laying of a sound basis for scientific and reflective thinking.

6. Giving the child the opportunities for developing manipulative skills, that will enable him or her to function effectively in the society, within the limits of his or her capacity.

7. Citizenship education as basis for effective participation in, and contributing to the society.

In order to achieve these set objectives, the 6-3-3-4 system was established with the most effective strategy adopted — **continuous assessment**.

The Problems

1. *Non-implementation*
There is need to correct the notion that the standard of education in Nigeria has not fallen. The truth is that, whereas, the standard, by way of policy and curriculum adjustment are getting higher, our level of attainment is declining very fast.

This is the consequence of our major problem — lack of implementation — which has continued to create obstacles in the improvement and advancement of our education.

Our inability to practically implement and not mentally theorise our commendable policy on education has created a vacuum in the physical, mental, and social educational development of our children, which has in the same degree affected economic development and moral advancement of the society.

Unless we are able to manifest physically what we have put down on paper, our attainment to visible higher standard of education, vis-à-vis, the society will be unrealistic.

We should bear in mind that this is the "Computer Age", when all aspects of life is rapidly advancing, giving rise to the need to re-orientate the child in his or her development. This is important, because a child's intelligence grows as much during the first four years of his or her life, as it does during the next thirteen years. Take for instance, continuous assessment.

Continuous Assessment

The continuous assessment method was aimed at exposing the children to diverse academic and creative activities that stimulate their intellect and emotion, to respond to their environment in all learning processes, thereby being able to fish out gifted/exceptional children, to integrate elements of special education into all "normal" schools, and to buttress each child's development of his or her mental and physical skills (talents).

This was to make possible, easy and quick assessment of the child's success in a particular skill or talent, that determines his or her placement in the 6-3-3-4 system under the educational categories of secondary, technical, vocational, and "special schools".

The 6-3-3-4 system was meant to see the child through an early educational development, such that, at the completion of primary education, he or she, through various developmental activities and continuous assessment must have made visible the innate skill or talent. Placed in the appropriate type of school as earlier mentioned, the child continues in the enhancement of this gifted talent, and specialises in this on graduation with a university/college degree. The child is then made mentally and physically skilful to contribute meaningfully to the nation.

Unfortunately, what obtains in our educational system today is the "test" system, in which series of tests are what is recorded as continuous assessment. This is a misinterpretation and misapplication of the term "continuous assessment" which render the talent of each child still very much undeveloped. Truly, there is a great difference between continuous assessment and testing.

The failings of this old system of testing was painfully pointed out in the *Handbook on Continuous Assessment*, published by the Federal Ministry of Education (page 7), as follows:

> One problem with this approach (testing) is that assessment is then directed mostly to the thought aspects of learning activities. Knowledge, understanding and other thinking skills acquired are evaluated and marks are awarded relative to the pupils' performances in the several subjects. Usually neglected in this procedure is the assessment of skills normally associated with both the character and the industry of the pupils.

This approach has made our numerous efforts in policy and curriculum reviews to have had no effect in classroom situations, therefore, no impact on the appropriate development of the children.

This our current exam-test system which grades the performance of the children to either pass or fail has blocked the development of children, such that, we are experiencing a lot of dropouts i.e. "unfit to go further", "truant of the worst order", "never do wells", "good for nothing children". This trend has its social and economic consequences with a high rate of illiteracy and immorality in the society.

It has to be emphasised here, that the purpose of continuous assessment is not to determine "pass" or "fail", but to discover the child's talents and capabilities, and direct him or her through the right channel for his or her self-fulfilment and national development.

2. *Non-availability of Facilities and Equipment*

There are fears in many quarters about the cost of provision of educational equipment and facilities to attain the objectives set by the programme stipulated in our National Policy on Education. The reasons for these fears shall be examined properly under financial problems.

Meanwhile, it should be stressed that the appropriate infrastructure, facilities, equipment and materials must be put in place for the implementation of this policy programme. Otherwise, we will continue to wallow in the muddy water of our educational system without any visible success but a decline and possible decay in our physical educational standard.

Inadequate instructional materials — textbooks, teaching aids, etc; poor physical facilities, dilapidated classroom buildings with leaking roofs, lack of toilet facilities and inadequate teacher/staff strength, will continue to pose serious educational problems. Consequently, our educational system will not evolve from the current testing system to continuous assessment system as desired and planned for.

How will the teacher assess the success in the development of the child if he or she has not the right teaching aid materials to engage the children in a variety of activities? How are the child's talents and capabilities going to be discovered? How can a child be comfortable and happy to learn in a harsh environment? Obviously, he or she will not want to go back to such an environment. Learning is supposed to be a pleasurable process for both the teacher and child (pupil) to experience.

Basically, our schools today have poor infrastructure and inadequate materials. An ill-equipped school does not wet the learning appetite of the child because it lacks the required stimulation to the different facets of human qualities. Nothing is of interest in school to the child who mistakenly thought he or she is a misfit and decides to drop out of school to go into an environment, where variety of activities are available for experimentation. To keep the child's attention on education, there must be activities that will catch his or her interest which will trigger the desire for a repeat experience. Thus, the desire to continue schooling is anchored.

The teachers are not left out in this issue. There must be facilities and equipment to help them continue to improve on their teaching knowledge. Some of the necessary equipment and materials for schools are discussed in chapter eight of this book.

3.   *Financial Problems*

When in 1986 a technical committee was set up by the National Council on Education to determine the reasons for the poor funding of primary education, leading to the collapse of our educational standard, the report concluded that the greatest problems of primary education in Nigeria are caused by three factors stemming from corruption.

These three factors were identified as:
a.   Misplacement of responsibility for primary education.
b.   Ineffective management and suppression.
c.   Diversion of the search funds to other uses.

The point here is not the inavailability of fund or the federal, state, and local government not financially being buoyant enough to fund primary education, but that of mismanagement, misappropriation and embezzlement of available fund, which would have been used to properly finance education in Nigeria.

As a result of corrupt practices, the government authorities responsible for primary and other levels of educational neglect or misplace this responsibility under the pretext that there is no fund. Most of the officials in whose hands the management and supervision of these funds are placed, do divert these funds to other uses that serve their self-interests by inventing gateways to siphoning the funds.

As recent as 1986, the Federal Government made a grant of ₦105 million available to assist in primary schools rehabilitation throughout the country. In considering the Political Bureau's Report, the Federal Government again in 1988, allocated ₦300 million directly to the local governments for various educational projects including primary schools rehabilitation. As a back-up fund, the ministry was also allocated ₦30 million to assist primary schools.

Where did these funds go? It is a question that yearns for a convincing answer because, the purposes for which these funds were allocated are yet to be seen in primary schools throughout the country.

It is conspicuously clear that all infrastructures and facilities in our schools today are in the worst state. Buildings have collapsed, leaving children to study under trees, exposing them to harsh weather conditions which pose a threat to their health.

Misappropriation and embezzlement of our educational funds have created artificial fund scarcity for financing our education programmes. These led to the imposition of tuition fees and other levies by the states, in spite of the Federal Government injunction that primary education shall be tuition free. Most of the states continued in this act secretly. What did they do with the large sum collected? Where is the money? The physical reality contradicts the assumed "good intention" for collecting these outrageous levies.

This has in no small measure affected the enrolment of children into primary schools, which rose from 8.3 million in 1976 when the Universal Primary Education (UPE) scheme was launched, to 16.5 million nationwide in 1983, and dropped to 13.3 million in 1986/87. Something has to be done as it is still dropping today.

Teachers' salaries are not spared from this unholy act of corruption as their salaries are either delayed or not paid for several months in the face of the present high cost of living, extended family commitments, and so on. There has been no incentives for teachers, no promotion, and no upgrading training opportunities, all leading to frustration, high level professional disenchantment, and boredom. The outcome of this is poor teaching activities and strikes that paralyse educational activities.

The re-launching of the Universal Primary Education in the form of Universal Basic Education (UBE) by the Federal Government on September 24, 1999, at Sokoto is a desired and welcome policy. There are still fears that the same draconian factor — corruption — which militated against its sustenance when earlier launched, is still going to be the stumbling block to the realisation of its effects on our educational system.

The new Universal Basic Education Policy, which makes education of the young children compulsory and free from primary school to junior secondary school 3 will succeed in solving some social and educational problems involving the children, if only the problems highlighted here are provided with solutions. They must be committedly redressed.

4. *Inconsistency in Education Policy*

Any major decision (policy) on education takes a period of at least twelve years for its impact to be felt in the society. This is only made possible if there is consistency in the policy and its implementation.

Because the policy is jettisoned before it is nurtured to maturity by successive governments, it is difficult to assess the potentiality of such policy whether it is good or bad.

Such has been the case in Nigeria. Government comes up with an applauded policy and just in the early stage of its implementation, it is discarded by a new government and a new policy is put in place to face the same fate as the previous one and the cycle continues. This is inconsistency which never produces any meaningful result and can't have any measurable impact on the society.

A goal can never be attained with an attitude of inconsistency, because inconsistency is a mother of impatience, that means you are neither achieving this nor that. We don't take out time to nurture our ideas and to allow them grow to maturity.

A policy is good or bad after grooming by way of practical

implementation, review, and modification. The truth is, no policy is good or bad, it all depends on when, how, where, and why it is being applied. Also important is who is doing the application, this is the co-ordination which the action or motion carries. If the "who" fails in action, it is not that the idea(s) or policy is bad, but it is simply a fault that needs to be addressed committedly.

Truly, the good aspect of a policy will be felt if appropriately implemented and given the opportunity to be reviewed, remodified and remodelled, in a sense, polished to meet the needs of every moment into the future. That a policy works today and doesn't work again tomorrow, is not a reason to discard it and tag it bad. All that is needed is to inject into it ideas which makes the policy fit into the prevailing situation and work. A policy should, therefore, evolve and this makes it dynamic. This evolution allows various ideas to be carried along, thereby improving on the policy and not abandoning it.

Our political uncertainty and instability, coupled with sectional sentiments, have led to imbalance and inconsistency in policy on education in Nigeria. Of course, the set goals couldn't have been attained with such "policy-making" in which everybody was not carried along. There is biased input in this case, which surely excluded some ideas that could help. This is a problem. A government comes and tilts the policy to the right to satisfy a sentiment, next time, another government takes over and again tilts the policy to the left to quench the thirst of another perceived sentiment, and this pendulum movement continues. To what end?

What is actually needed is an evolving policy that will continue to take into consideration every educational need of every segment of the society. A balanced policy, so to say, devoid of any kind of sentiment, for every segment of the society is important and has something to contribute to the welfare and growth of the nation.

5. *Day/Boarding Schools*

It is believed that the initial intention for establishing boarding schools was to create a conducive and enabling environment for young children to learn. In addition, such environment permits concentration, co-operation, creativity and a school culture that aids students to socialise without being violent.

The emotional, mental and physical aspects of the children are being developed, and their behaviour moulded to a better one. The students then were made to learn and learn well, because the schools were well equipped with materials for teaching and learning, infrastructures were in good working conditions. Disciplinary measures were always taken wherever necessary to properly direct the unruly, prepare the mind of the child to what ought to be done in the learning process. The results were disciplined children aspiring to do better to become responsible adults in the society.

Indeed, one is tempted to agree that those who are products of that system or programme of education are better adults now, as compared with the products of today's education system or programme, in terms of acquired educational knowledge.

Some portions of our education problem may be attributed to the introduction of day-school system. The introduction of this programme in the late '70s was to enable parents, who could not afford the cost of a boarding school, send their children to school at a reduced cost. Secondly, to reduce the high rate of illiteracy and with time eradicate it completely. It is for these same reasons that more secondary schools were built and brought close to every community.

This is a worthy ideal but what is wrong is its implementation; it has been overdone, such that, we are almost having system of total day schooling. The boarding system has been de-emphasised to a fault. Only the government owned Unity Schools and some privately owned schools offer this arrangement at a very high cost with destructive competition amongst parents who can afford it. The best children don't get admission into these Unity Schools, only children of "money-bags", no matter the low score in the entrance examination. These boarding schools are few in number.

Taking a critical look at the day school system, it could be said that it has outlived the aims of embarking on it, because it has over the years not succeeded in reducing the illiteracy rate, and school attendance rate has also not increased. The reverse has been the case in our society. Rather, the day school system has succeeded in destroying the children, enslaving them and exposing them to all sorts of social vices.

The children have been taken away from the "school culture" that used to be and dumped into the "rude society" with their unguided minds and left at the mercy of "cruel games" imitation of social adults, only to become irresponsible adults terrorising the society. They have been deprived of appropriate educational development through a prescribed learning process.

The difference is boldly clear; the children in these few Government (Unity) Schools, with adequate teaching materials, qualified, well-paid teachers, and good infrastructures, cannot be compared with those in public schools with "rotten" environments called schools. If 30% of the children in Unity Schools are having behaviour disorders, 70% of the children in poor public schools are having these same behaviour disorders.

In the name of day school, children are made to learn more social activities full of distractions than educational activities. What do we expect?

The day school system which is being practised in the developed nations, is right and successful there because of their residential set-up that limits the child's public interaction while at home. The child's public interaction may be made possible during visits to places of interest with parent or guardians. Otherwise, his or her relationship is more of "home-school", while gradually being exposed to the larger society.

This is a different situation in Nigeria, where residential areas are over crowded with loose children playing wildly about, street hawking and so on. The children are not environmentally protected to create a conducive learning environment only those from rich parents enjoy such privilege. The gap is so wide.

In as much as our goals are on focus, to reduce illiteracy rate, conscious efforts must be made to reorganise the day-boarding school system, such that, it has a balanced effect. Let most public secondary schools provide boarding facilities, so that average income parents who can afford the cost can send their children. Out of intense desire to educate their children, many parents are willing to sacrifice their scarce resources to fulfil this desire but because of the poor behaviour and performances of these children due to some environmental influences, these parents are discouraged and withdrawn.

Meanwhile, a guided environment, such as the boarding facility can improve the children's behaviours and performances, thereby encouraging such parent.

More boarding facilities must be provided enough to avoid the corrupt practice of "buying grades" for admission. Government can subsidise a percentage of the boarding fee as part of the free education scheme.

It is very necessary that our children are guided rightly at early age and educated under such close guidance, to become responsible adults in future to lead the nation to growth and development only through competent, meticulous and honest implementation of a dynamic and balanced policy on education. Can this opportunity be provided for the development of the child? It is their right.

REFERENCES

Broudy, H.S. 1961. *Building a Philosophy of Education*. Englewood Cliffs, N.J.: Prentice Hall Inc.

Bruner, J. 1960. *The Process of Education*. Cambridge, Mass: Harvard University Press.

Fafunwa, A.B. 1969. "The Purpose of Teacher Education." In Adaralegbe, A.(ed). *A Philosophy for Nigerian Education*. Lagos: Heinemann Educational Books (Nig.) Ltd.

Federal Republic of Nigeria. 1998. *National Policy on Education*. Lagos: NERDC Press.

Hook, S. 1964. *Education for Modern Man*. New York: The Dial Press.

Marler, C.D. 1975. *Philosophy and Schooling*. Boston: Allyn & Bacon, Inc.

Obinidike, O.E. 1980. *The Foundations of Philosophy of Education*. Jos: University Press.

Ogunsanya, S. 1988. *The Teaching Profession*. Ibadan: Laville Publications.

Phenix, P.H. 1964. "The Architectonics of Knowledge." In S. Elam (ed.). *Education and the structure of knowledge*. Chicago: Rand McNally & Co.

Schwab, J.J. 1964. "Problems, Topics, and Issues." In S. Elam (ed). *Education and the Structure of Knowledge*. Chicago: Rand McNally & Co.

Chapter Eight

EQUIPMENT AND MATERIALS FOR SCHOOLS

Equipment and Materials

Equipment and materials have a major influence on both staff members and children. Consequently, the task of deciding on specific equipment and materials should be determined by the educational objective. They should be planned and budgeted for at the conception of the educational programmes. This will enable the appropriate architectural structure to be put in the place that fits the type of equipment and materials required. That is, the building and infrastructures must be designed according to the equipment and materials to be used in that school.

Purchasing Guidelines

It is very important to consider certain factors when purchasing equipment and materials for school programmes. Because of items that do not meet the needs of the programmes or are insufficient in quality for the activities planned, they hamper, rather than facilitate early child education.

The quality of the equipment and materials is to be insured and thus, lengthens the time for replacement. In today's inflationary world, careful planning is essential if the items are to be secured within budgetary limitations.

For this reason, only equipment and materials that will facilitate meeting the educational objectives are to be purchased. Sequenced materials are needed after programme instruction; self-correcting materials, materials that encourage creativity, materials for handicapped children, and materials to teach multicultural and non-sexist concepts. Items must be appropriate and usefulness is of prime importance.

To avoid duplications and to make sure essential items have priority, list of inventory should be maintained. Durable and relatively maintenance-free equipment and materials should be selected. Because both budget and space are limited, materials that are comprehensive in nature should be purchased, such as, materials that can be used in a variety of situations that are suitable for individual differences. These sort of materials stimulate creativity.

Equipment and materials that are aesthetically pleasing and appealing to senses should be selected because children love the awareness of colour, texture, size, form, brightness, sound, etc.

When purchasing items, it should be remembered that children are to be active participants and not spectators. Therefore, equipment and materials that actively involve children are to be purchased. Records should be kept for incoming and outgoing items, damaged items, items to be replaced or repaired, and other conditions of items.

In the case of caring for equipment and materials, children should be taught how to care for these items because this teaches them good habits and helps prevent expensive repairs and replacements as a result of damages caused by the children. Staff members should also join in checking, cleaning and maintaining these equipment and materials.

Specific Equipment and Materials
Most of the specific equipment and materials used in early child education are instructional, these are representations of everyday life and have been produced or selected for their educational relevance. Some of the necessary ones are as discussed below:

Furniture
Furniture for young children should be of proper height and proportions, durable and lightweight, and have rounded corners. If space is at a premium, furniture, especially children's chairs, should be stackable. Tables accommodating from four to six children are advisable for kindergartens

and nursery schools. Rectangular tables are better because they accommodate large pieces of paper for art and craft work, while round tables are attractive in the library.

Specifications
1. Chairs should have a broad base to prevent ripping and a full saddle seat with a back support approximately 20 cm above the seat.
2. Chair weight should not exceed 4 to 4.5 kg.
3. Distance between the seat height of the chairs and the table surface should be approximately 19 cm.
4. Chairs used as tables should not have arms.

In addition, the activity room must be equipped with storage units and dividers. Staff members should have comfortable furniture, work surfaces for making instructional aids and places for filing and storing records and other materials. Furniture should be suited to the children's physical development and the programme. Some of the required furniture might be:

- Adult chairs
- Adult rocking chair
- Children's rocking chairs, easy chairs, stools, or benches
- Children's table (39-50 cam high)
- Filing cabinets
- Flag
- Pencil sharpener
- Portable or built-in children's cubbies
- Portable dividers (bulletin boards, chalkboards, or screens)
- Staff members' desk or table
- Staff members' locker or cupboard
- Staff members' cubbies for mail
- Stapler
- Waste basket

Audio-visual Equipment

These equipment, though used for early education programme are not substitutes for real experiences, but they are helpful in the learning process. Audio-visual equipment that might be needed include:
- Camera (35mm and/or Polaroid)
- Filmstrip projector and filmstrips
- Headsets or earphones and listening stations
- "Language master"
- Loop (8mm)
- Movie projector (16mm) and film
- Overhead projector and transparencies
- Projection table
- Record player and records
- Screen (91 x 122cm)
- Slide projectors and slides
- Stereoscope and stereoscope reels (view master)
- Still pictures and graphic representations
- Storage cabinets for tapes, slides etc
- Tape recorders (cassette and/or reel-to-reel) and blank tapes
- Television
- Three-dimensional models
- Videotape equipment

Micro-computers

It has been recognised that computer literacy — awareness of the uses and limitations of computers as to what they are, how they work, and their impact in our lives — is no longer a skill needed only in certain professions but also in the field of education. It has then become very necessary to infuse computer literacy objective into the curriculum. Because micro-computers are a relatively new educational topic, some basic facts in relation to early child education will have to be looked into.

Using and understanding micro-computer involve learning the technical language. Such language like **logo** which means "word" in Greek, was developed by Seymour Papery and members of the Massachusetts Institute of Technology to enable young children to think by programming computers. In programming, children must plan and test ideas following a logical sequence. The language begins with graphics but extends through the entire range of mathematical and logic operations, using robots and sound.

Approaches to instruction as provided by Computer-Assisted Instruction (CAI) are many and care should be taken to select programmes that fit the needs. Computer-Assisted Instruction (CAI) can take the following forms:

1. *Drill and Practice*

This is the common form of CAI meant to be used to reinforce classroom learning in areas such as, spelling, mathematical facts and facts learned in subjects such as history and geography. This approach is practical for increasing speed and efficiency in routine learning situation, but it is not meant to replace classroom instructions for understanding.

2. *Tutorial Approach*

This approach of CAI is designed so that a child can test his or her understanding of a topic. The format is such that, the child works at his or her own rate and gain mastery of the content.

3. *Games*

This uses a problem-solving format such as searching for a number or alphabet as the computer gives clues. This type of game helps a child learn the sequence of letters and numbers in a game format. Other games may be similar to "monopoly", where the player must deploy his or her resources well to achieve a goal.

4. *Simulation*

This CAI approach uses the characteristics of a real situation (e.g. landing on the moon or an economic depression) where children can make decisions and can note the consequences.

5. *Writing and Graphic*

CAI can involve computer editing and revising writings and displays of graphic art.

6. *Computer Programming*

CAI can involve computer programming where the child controls the machine and deals with model building.

The use of micro-computer helps the child to think creatively. Many of these CAI programme approaches are mostly combined.

Guidelines for Selecting Micro-computer Equipment
Selecting of micro-computers for educational purpose must be based on goals and objectives. The technical skills of the staff members in using the micro-computer and the availability of service centres to provide in-depth maintenance, must be taken into consideration.

Hardware and Software must be purchased together because the programmes are often machine-specific i.e. fit a particular computer.

In purchasing computer hardware, it is wise to project future needs, therefore, model that meets the needs of today as well as tomorrow is the best.

Interest Centres
These are centres well equipped with equipment and materials for educational purposes of young children. This could be situated either in the school premises or in community neighbourhood accessible to young school children. Equipment and materials that may be found in these centres are classified according to programmes for the child's development.

Language Arts
The equipment and materials needed for language arts are for the specific curricular areas of listening, speaking, preparation for reading, writing and literature. Items needed include:
- Alphabet letters (alphabet insets, kinaesthetic letters, letters to step on, etc) books and recordings of stories
- Filmstrips and/or slides of children's stories
- Flannel board
- Lotto (covering many subjects)
- Objects and pictures depicting rhyming words or initial sounds
- Perceptual and conceptual development games (absurdities, missing pats, sequencing dominoes)
- Pictures and graphic representations of finger plays, poems, and stories puppets and a puppet theatre
- Puzzles (jigsaw, sequencing, etc) and puzzle rack

Equipment and Materials for Schools 169

- Recordings of sounds, such as animals, city, and home sounds and home
- Sounds; home sounds and home
- Signs and labels
- Typewriter

Mathematics

Concepts frequently taught in Mathematics include numbers, number combinations, numerals, geometric concepts, size, position, and patterns. Mathematics centre can be separately established in school if need be. Equipment and materials that help children in their mathematical development are:

- Abacus (or counting frame)
- Balance scales for developing an understanding of simple
- number operations
- Beads for pattern work and for developing an understanding of geometric concepts
- "Broad Stair" for developing size concepts
- Calendars, thermometers, clocks, scales, etc, that have numerals
- Counting discs
- "Cuisenaire" materials for developing number and geometric concepts
- Cylinders which are graduated in diameter and/or height
- Design cubes
- Dowel rods in graduated lengths, for developing serial concepts; fabric, wall paper, cabinet and floor covering samples for pattern work, flannel board object, numerals
- Fraction plates or cards
- Geometric shape insets and solids
- "Golden Beads" for developing place value concepts
- Lotto (number and geometric shapes)
- Measuring (cards, insets, kinaesthetic, puzzles, numerals to step on etc.)
- Objects to count
- Pegboards and pegs for developing number and geometric concepts
- Picture books, illustrations, poems, and finger plays which have mathematical concepts, pictures of objects for grouping into sets and of geometric shapes "Pink Tower" for developing size concepts.

- Sorting box for geometric shapes
- Stacking and nesting blocks for developing size concepts
- Unit blocks and/or parquetry blocks for developing geometric and size concepts

Social Studies
Home and family, community workers, concepts from geography, sociology and economics are frequently covered in social studies. Items needed are books, poems, and finger plays with the following themes:

1. Home and family
2. Community workers
3. Self awareness (need for security, self confidence, achievement belonging to groups, etc.)
4. Holidays and
5. Family living in other parts of the world

- Doll house, dolls, and miniature furniture
- Globe and maps (primary globe and a simple map of the area)
- Holiday decorations (although most decorations are child made)
- Picture, posters, and flannel boards with the following themes: Home and family, community workers; people in other parts of the country and in other parts of the world; various geographical land and water areas and holidays
- Puppets (family, community workers and holiday characters such as Santa Claus)
- Puzzles and lotto family, community workers, and holidays
- Village (miniature)

Blocks and Building Structures
These may be set up as indoor or outdoor activities with the following materials

100 units	4 x 7 x 14cm
180 double units	4 x 7 x 28cm
200 quadruple units	4 x 7 x 56cm
36 ramps	4 x 7 x 14cm

25 roof boards   1 x 7 x 28cm
10 curves (elliptical)   4 x 7 x 35cm
10 curves (circular)   4 x 7 x 20cm
10 Y-Switches   4 x 21 x 28cm
20 cylinder   7cm diam x 14cm
20 pillar   4 x 4 x 14cm
25 half-unit   4 x 7 x 7cm
20 pairs triangles   4 x 7 x 7cm

House-keeping and Dramatic Play
Children in this dramatic play act out the roles of family members and community workers, school activities and story plots, and learn social behaviours such as table manners and telephone courtesy. Equipment and materials for this purpose are:

- Costumes, especially hats and tools of the trade (e.g. doctor's bag and stethoscope) of community workers and costumes for re-enacting stories, doll items (table and two to four chairs, doll furniture bed or cradle, carriage, chest of drawers, refrigerator, stove, sink, cabinet for dishes, dish washer, dryer, stool, wardrobes linens, pots, pans, dishes, flatware (all items should be unbreakable); ironing board and iron; house keeping articles — broom, dust mop, dust pan, and dust rag; artificial food; clothes line, clothes pines, and dish pan)
- Dolls (baby and teenage dolls)
- Dress-up clothes for men and women (long skirts, blouses, dresses, shirts, pants, shoes, caps, hats, boots, small suitcase, scarves and ribbons, flower, jewelleries, purses, necklaces, and pieces of materials)
- Fabric (several strips two or three yards in length, which can be used imaginatively)
- Gadgets, such as rubber hose, steering wheels, pipe, old faucets, door locks, springs, keys, pulleys, bells, scales, alarm clock, cash register and play money, cartons and
- Miniature doll house, community, farm, service stations, etc.
- Mirrors (full-length and hand-held)

- Play screens, cardboard houses, etc.
- Puppets and stages
- Rocking chair
- Stuffed animals
- Telephone

Science

Both biological and physical science concepts are presented to young children. Because of the diversity of science equipment and materials, they are not all stored. Some of them are:

- Animals and insect cages (container for small insects, cocoon holder, cage with tread mill, rabbit hutch, container for praying mantis, large walk-in-cage, etc)
- Animals, insects and fish
- Aquarium (equipped with air pump and hose, filter, gravel, fish, net, light, thermometer, medicine and remedies, and aquarium guide)
- Balloons
- Birds and suet feeders, and bird house
- Books and pictures with the following themes; animals, plants, natural phenomena, machinery, bubble pipes and soaps
- Equipment
- Butterfly net
- Chick incubator
- Collections (rocks, bird nest, insects, sea shells, etc)
- Colour wheel, colour paddles (i.e. glass or plastic paddles in the primary colours) and prisms
- Compass
- Dry cell batteries, flashlight bulbs, bells, light receptacle, and electrical wire
- Gardening tools (child-sized)
- Kaleidoscope
- Magnets (bar, horseshoe, etc.)
- Magnifying glasses (hand-held and tripod)
- Measuring equipment (measuring cups and spoons, scales, balances, bathrooms posters, time instruments, sum dial, egg time, clocks, thermometers ideal for indoor/outdoor and play) and linear measuring instruments (English and metric)

- Miscellaneous materials (string, tape, hot plate, bottles of assorted sizes, pans, buckets, sponges, and hardware gadgets)
- Model animals, space equipment, machine, solar system, etc
- Pin wheels
- Plants, seeds and bulbs (with planting pots, soil, fertiliser, and watering cans)
- Pulleys and gear
- Puzzles on science themes
- Seed box
- Wheel barrows (child-size)
- Sound producing objects
- Terrariums
- Weather vane

Water, Sand and Mud

These are found both in the indoor and outdoor areas and some of the items for activities relating to water, sand and mud are:

- Mops and sponges for cleaning up
- Sand (white and brown)
- Sand and mud, toy trucks, jeeps, trains, bulldozer, tractors, captions can, gelatine or sand moulds, cookie cutters, spoons, pans, cups, dishes, strainers, watering cans, shovels, block, sand dools, sieves, pitchers, sand pails, lades, sifters, screens, sand combs, planks, and rocks)
- Sand table
- Siphons tubes
- Soap (floating) and soap flakes
- Straws
- Water play table
- Water play toys (small pitchers, watering cans, measuring cups, bowls of various sizes, plastic bottles, detergent squeeze bottles, medicine droppers, funnels, strainers, hose corks, squeeze bottles, sponges, washable dolls, wire shirks, butter churns, and shaving brushes)
- Water pump for indoor water table cooking

Children are occasionally provided opportunity to have cooking experiences and for this, kitchen facility is provided in schools with needed equipment and materials as follows:

- Baking pans (cookie sheets, muffin tins, cake pans and pie pans)
- Dish cloth and dish towels
- Dishes and flatwares
- Electric, countertop oven, boiler
- Hot plate
- Kitchen utensils (stirring spoons, spatula, tongs, and paring knife)
- Measuring spoons and cups
- Mixing bowls
- Napkins
- Pitcher, serving dishes, basket and tray
- Place mats, popcorn popper
- Pot holders
- Recipes written for young children
- Sauce pans
- Serving cart equipped with wheels
- Skillet
- Tea kettle

Wood-work or Carpentry
Wood-work or carpentry interest centre or workshop may be set up in either indoor or outdoor area. This is a popular centre for young children. Equipment and materials needed are:

- Variety of clamps
- Cloth, leather, styrofoam, cardboard, cork, bottles, caps, and other scraps to nail on wood
- Hand drill
- Glue
- Hammers (claw) of differing weights and sizes
- Magnets (tied to a string for picking up dropped nails)
- Nails (thin nails with good sized-heads, because thick nails tend to split wood)
- Paints (water base)

- Pencils (heavy, soft-lead)
- Pliers
- Ruler and yardstick are used as a straight edge, more than for measuring sandpaper of various grades (wrapped around and tacked to blocks)
- Sawhorses
- Saws (crosscut and coping)
- Scraps of wood (soft woods such as white pine, poplar, fir, and basswood with no knots), dowel, wood slates, and wooden spools.
- Soap (rubbed across the sides of a saw to male it slide easier)
- Tacks
- Tri-square
- Vices (attached to workbench)
- Wire (hand-pliable)
- Worktable or Workbench (drawers for sandpaper and nails are desirable)

Music
Children respond to music by listening, singing, playing rhythm instruments and dancing. Items needed are:

- Autoharp
- Capes and full skirts for dancing
- Chromatic bells
- Chromatic pitch pipe
- Headsets and listening stations
- Music books for singing, rhythms, and appreciation
- Music cart
- Piano and piano bench
- Pictures of musical instruments and dancers
- Record rack or cabinet and/or cassette rack
- Records and cassettes
- Rhythm instruments (drum, calves, triangles, tambourines, cymbals, toms, hand bells, jingle sticks, wrist bells, ankle bells, shakers, maracas, rhythm sticks, tone blocks, castanets, sand blocks).
- Sounder, finger cymbals and gong bell

- Scarves
- Stories (e.g. picture books) about music and sound
- Tape recorder
- Xylophone

Art

Using various art media, children create graphic and three-dimensional works. They learn concepts of colour, form, texture and size. Equipment and materials needed are:
- Apron or smock (snaps preferred, because ties can knot)
- Chalk (various colours)
- Clay and clay-boards
- Colour paddles (three paddles; red, yellow and blue)
- Crayons (red, yellow, orange, green, purple, black and brown)
- Display boards and tables
- Drying rack
- Easels (two working sides with a tray holding paint containers on each side)
- Erasers (art gum and felt for chalkboard)
- Geometric shapes (insets, etc.)
- Gummed paper in assorted shapes for making designs and pictures
- Junk materials for collage work (beads, buttons, cellophane, cloth, flat corks, wall paper scraps, wrapping paper scraps and yam)
- Magazines for collage
- Markers (felt tip, various colour)
- Mosaics
- Mounting board (5.39 cm x 12.19 cm)
- Pails (plastic with covers for storing clay)
- Paint (powdered or premixed tempera paint in various colours)
- Paint jars
- Paint and varnish brushes
- Paper (corrugated paper; newsprint 61 x 91 cm, finger paint paper or glazed shelf paper construction, tissue, and poster papers of various colours, manila paper; 46 x 61 cm, metallic paper; 25 x 33 cm, wrapping Paper and tag board; 61 x 91 cm)
- Paper bags

- Paper cutter
- Paste, brushes and sticks
- Paste and glue
- Pictures of children engaging in art activities and of famous artists
- Printing blocks or stamps
- Recipes for finger paint, modelling materials, etc.
- Reproductions of famous paintings and pictures of sculpture and architecture
- Ruler
- Scissors
- Scissors rack
- Sorting boxes for sorting colours and shapes
- Staff members' supplies (art gum erasers, masking, cellophane, and mystic tapes, liquid starch, dish washing detergent, straight pins, shears, stapler, paper punch and cutter)
- Stories and poems with themes of colour, shapes, size, beauty of nature, etc.
- Textured materials
- Yarn (various colours)
- Needles

Manipulative Activities

These types of activities help children develop eye-hand co-ordination. Equipment and materials for these are:

- Balls (inflatable; 36 cm, 22 and 13 cm in diameters)
- Beanbags
- Blocks (hollow and/or large floor blocks)
- Bridges (platform)
- Doll carriages
- Gardening tools
- Horizontal ladder
- Horse (broom-stock variety)
- Inner tubes (rubber)
- Jumping boards
- Jungle gym (approximately 1.62 cm high)

- Keys (wooden)
- Ladder box
- Ladies (cleats or hooks on each end)
- Mattresses for jumping (innerspring)
- Packing cases (wooden; 107 cm x 76 x76 cm)
- Pedal toys (e.g. tricycles)
- pictures of children playing and people engaging in physical activities and sports
- Planks (cleats at ends to hold place on climbing structure)
- Platform and step
- Ring toss game and rings
- Rocking boats
- Rope (jumping, 3.05 cm long)
- Sand pit
- Sand play toys
- Sawhorses
- Seesaw
- Singing game recordings
- Slide
- Stories with physical activity themes
- Swing with canvas seats or tire swings
- Wagons (and other pull/ride-in toys)
- Walking beam
- Walking boards
- Water play equipment

Handicapped Children

A growing number of materials are being designed for children with a variety of disabilities. Many types of handicaps require therapy with equipment and materials that can only be handled by a trained professional. The less severely handicapped children can still use equipment and material for "normal" children. However, "special" children actually need different equipment and materials for comfort, safety and for therapy. Basic equipment are:

- Carrel
- Chairs designed for specific handicap
- Matting (non-slip)

- Tables designed for use with wheelchairs and other chairs for handicapped.
- Trays for work and play (used in place of table or countertop)
- Walkers

Perceptual-motor Equipment and Materials

These are basic needs of most handicapped children. Skills are usually subdivided into gross and fine perceptual motor tasks. These equipment and materials are:

- Dot-to-dot sheets
- Drawing and writing equipment (e.g. chalkboards)
- Dressing frames and vests
- Feeling boxes, bags, etc.
- Figure-ground cards and charts
- Form boards
- Lacing cards
- Montessori didactic (sensory) materials
- Nesting and stacking equipment
- Parquetry (large)
- Pegs and pegboards
- Puzzles
- Sandpaper numerals and letters
- Scissors
- Tracing stencils and templates

Raw or Primitive Materials

These are materials that do not duplicate reality:
- A lump of clay
- A scrap of cloth
- A bead, etc.

These are excellent for instruction because children with various degrees of competence and differing interests can use them and also because these materials permit children to use various symbols to stand for real objects.

Community Resources (Excursion)

Taking children to the community through field or study trips (excursions), bringing the community to the children through resource people, help socialise the children and create awareness of the society.

Outstanding persons in the community or society should be made to have opportunity of addressing the children to inspire them to achieving greater heights. The staff members should compile a list of places to visit and of resource people suitable to the school programmes and make proper arrangement.

The list of places may include:
- Airport
- Art and craft museums
- Bakery
- Bank
- Beauty shop
- Brickyard
- Buildings under construction
- Dairy
- Dentist's office
- Doctor's office
- Fast food chain
- Pizza shop
- Vocational high school (class and equipment in cosmetology, mechanics, graphics etc.)
- Dry cleaner's shop
- Electric company
- Elementary school
- Farm (tree, animal and crop)
- Feed store
- Fields
- Fire station
- Gas company
- Grocery store (all comers' market and supermarket)
- Hospital
- Ice cream plant

Equipment and Materials for Schools 181

- Library
- Manufacturing companies
- Milk processing plant
- Neighbourhood walk
- Newspaper office
- Parks (neighbourhood, city, state or national)
- Pet shop
- Photography studio
- Police station
- Post office
- Telephone company
- Television cable company
- Water plant
- Zoo

Professional Library

There should be a professional library, mainly for the teachers and school staff members, to keep them up-to-date, informed and help them in their planning. The library should therefore contain the following:
- Journal, newsletters and special publications of professional organisations concerned with young children
- Instructional manuals in addition to those regularly used
- Curriculum guides printed by the state board of education, state department of public welfare, local school system and other early childhood programmes that have similar objectives
- Professional books and audiovisuals concerned with various aspects of early childhood: child development, curriculum, guidance and administration.
- Catalogues and brochures from distributors of equipment and materials
- Newsletters of information on current legislation pertaining to child care and education
- Information from local community resources: health department, dental association, sickle cell anaemia and other groups
- Bibliographies of pertinent topics in child development, care and education, and parenting skills.

Recreational Facilities for Schools

The following are recreational facilities that are supposed to be made available and maintained at all educational levels; primary, secondary, and tertiary, in order to develop the athletic and sporting talents of young children and youths.

All primary schools should be provided with:
- Athletic equipment
- Football pitch
- Volleyball court
- Handball facilities
- Basketball facilities

All secondary, vocational/technical schools should be provided with:
- Athletics equipment
- Football Pitch
- Volleyball court
- Handball facilities
- Table tennis Court
- Lawn tennis Court
- Basket ball Court
- Cricket facilities
- Hockey facilities

All tertiary institutions should be provided with all sporting facilities, including a swimming pool, a mini stadium and indoor games facilities.

REFERENCES

Agun, I. 1988. "Learning materials towards education in the year 2000." *Journal of Educational Media Technology,* 1(4): 498-521.

Combs, A.W. 1978. "Humanism, Education and the Future". *Educational Leadership,* 35(4): 300-303.

Ezeocha, P.A. 1985. *School Management and Supervision.* Owerri: New Africa Publishing Co. Ltd.

Goodlad, J.I. 1975. *The Dynamics of Educational Change*. New York: McGraw-Hill.

Hencley, S. and Yates, J. (eds). 1974. *Futurism in Education*. Berkeley: McCutchan Publishing Co.

Ikerionwu, J.C. 2000. "Importance of Aids and Resources in Classroom Teaching." In A.M. Oyeneyin (ed.). *Perspectives on Classroom Teaching I*. Abuja: Martmonic Press.

Lowman, J. 1987. *Mastering the Techniques of Teaching*. New Delhi: Prentice-Hall of India Private Ltd.

Mkpa, M.A. 1988. "Status of Implementation of the National Policy as it Relates to Instructional Materials". In E.T. Ehiametchor, Izuagie, M.A. and Okitan, S.O. (eds.). *Implementation of National Policy on Education: Theoretical and Empirical Analyses*. Lagos: Longman.

Nwagbara, A.C. and Ikegulu, B.O. 1994. "Development of Instructional Materials in the Implementation of Comprehensive Population/ Family Life Education Programming in Nigeria". *Perspective in Population Education*, 3: 11-16.

Obanya, P.A.I. 1989. "Potentialities of educational materials in Africa." *Inter Learning of Educational Innovation*, 6:55-64.

Ofoegbu, L.I. 1992. *Teaching Aids and Resources*. Lagos: Nelson Publishers Ltd.

Ogunranti, A. 1985. *Problems and Prospects of Educational Technology in Nigeria*. Ibadan: Heinemann Educational Books (Nig.) Ltd.

Okoh, N. 1983. (ed.). *Professional Education: A Book of Readings*. Benin City: Ethiope Publishing Co.

Onwuegbu, O.I. 1979. *Discover Teaching*. Enugu: Fourth Dimension Publishing Co. Ltd.

Chapter Nine

FINANCING AND BUDGETING

Financing and Managing

The financing of education in Nigeria began with the two major religious bodies, Christianity and Islam, which established schools in the southern and northern parts of Nigeria respectively.

The early Christian missionaries in the south started mission schools to teach their converts how to read and write, and these schools they funded. Likewise, in the north Arabic schools were opened to teach the reading and writing of Arabic language and they were funded by the Islamic body.

The first government intervention in financing education actually began in 1882, when the British government promulgated the first education ordinance which covered the West African territories. This empowered colonial governments to open schools and this made it possible for such schools to receive grants-in-aid.

It was from this time government started funding education in Nigeria. This funding has taking various forms, such as the introduction of school fees and Parent Teachers Association, P.T.A. levies, and the Universal Primary Education which introduced free education, first in the western region in 1955, and later in the eastern region in 1956. School enrolment increased tremendously, leading to financial burden on these regional governments. At a point the introduction of free education was accepted as a mistake because of the inability of government to finance the scheme, so it failed.

In the north, the approach to education funding was quite different. They continued to finance education with government of the northern region's grants and school fees. Education funds were not diverted to non-educational purposes.

The Federal Government by the end of 1971 took over mission schools, thereby added to the financial burden on education. It later felt that national unity, tolerance and understanding would be brought about by education, and so reintroduced the Universal Primary Education scheme in 1976.

The Federal Government was to fund the whole programme, while the state and local governments were to implement it. There were loopholes for wastage as the management mechanism was neither streamlined nor was it properly supervised or co-ordinated. For as long as the oil boom existed and the federal government paid primary education bills, the faults of chaotic management were not obvious.

In the third national development plan (1973-1980), government's financial investment in education amounted to 2.5 billion Naira. But when the civilian government came in 1979, the federal government withdrew completely its subsidy for primary education and transferred the responsibility to the local governments. This effectively put an end to UPE in most states. When the military took over in 1984, the UPE scheme was completely put to rest as this became a nationwide affair. So, school fees and levies were once again introduced in all states. The states and local governments were to fund education with less than 15% of their revenues.

Presently, the government's mode of financing education is deplorable. Despite an increase in government financial support, it is hardly adequate to meet even the recurrent cost left to capital cost. Of this recurrent cost, teachers' salaries remain the dominant item which the three tiers of government hardly meet up. This lack of payment of teachers' salaries has led to many nationwide strikes. It became worst when the Federal Government changed the revenue formula, increasing the share of the local governments and allowing a reduction of the federal share.

With this, the Federal Government handed over to the local governments, full financial responsibility for operating primary schools in the country. The local governments, since then, have been unable to meet this obligation. Many of them do divert education funds to non-educational projects.

Various measures have been devised to raise funds, such as per capital levies on pupils for development, survival, equipment, and registration. Taxable adults pay education rates. Yet, these measures have proved ineffective to arrest their insufficient funds situation. Primary education, as such, is on the verge of collapse.

In 1988, the government in an attempt to rescue the poor state of primary education came up with a fourteen point policy on management and financing education in the country.

The policy stated thus:

1. There was an urgent need to salvage primary education, federal participation would be in the highest national interest and consistent with the present constitutional injunctions and divisions of responsibility.
2. Since salaries constituted the largest single item of change in primary education, any meaningful assistance in support of the level will have to address primary school staff salaries.
3. The Federal Government will contribute annually to a fund; 65% of the calculated cost of primary school salaries. This fund, to be known as "The National Primary Education Fund" is to be taken directly from the Federal Government's own share of the federation account.
4. 20% of the fund contribution will be kept aside regularly for a period of 10 years for twelve educationally disadvantaged states, which had been identified by the Armed Forces Ruling Council (AFRC), for the purpose of primary education development.
5. 80% of the fund to be deducted from the Federal Government's share of the federation account will be shared among the 21 states plus Abuja, for the purpose of salaries of teaching and non-teaching staff.
6. The sharing among the states in both instances shall be on the basis of:
    a. Equality of the states
    b. The total population of each state
7. In view of the importance of the joint participation of all to the success of this policy, each state is required to set aside its own contribution, to which the Federal Government will add its own.

Financing and Budgeting 187

8. Similarly, each local government area will set aside its own contribution to which the joint federal and state fund will be added.
9. Appropriate provisions will be made to ensure that each tier make its own contribution and that funds are passed to the local governments, and at that level, used specifically for the purpose of primary education.
10. The mechanism for management of this entire scheme are being worked out, including the setting up by decree of the funds referred to above.
11. The setting up by decree of a National Commission of Primary Education, a parastatal of the Federal Ministry of Education that will have the principal responsibility of advising the Federal Government on the amount to be deducted each year for the specified purposes and for allocating it to the designated agencies of the states and any other appropriate agency as directed by the Federal Government.
12. Development of primary education will however be at the state and local government levels, particularly at the local government level. Each tier (state or local government), would need to set up a specific mechanism for funding and management of primary education i.e. State Primary Schools Management Board and Local Education Authority. Money will not be released to any state that has not set up this mechanism.
13. Advisory committees on primary education will also be provided for at the district and village levels.
14. When this scheme takes off in January, 1989, it is expected that the federal contribution of almost 2/3 of primary school wages, and the setting up of appropriate uniform mechanism would once and for all, solve the problem of funding and management of primary education, as well as remove the divisive problem of education imbalance from its very foundation: primary education.

This policy has since then been implemented but the problems in financing and managing primary education persisted. These problems are the same in secondary and tertiary institutions in Nigeria. In spite of the huge financial investment said to have been pumped into the educational system, the dream of attaining a high standard, well-equipped educational system has turned to a nightmare. The system is manifesting gross shortage of everything.

In some schools, buildings are not maintained, children study under trees, teaching aids, books and furniture are lacking, and teachers are laid-off to save costs. The system is on the verge of total collapse.

Education Tax Decree No. 7 of 1993
It was to grapple with the escalating problems of financing education in Nigeria and to arrest the imminent collapse of the system that government in response to the recommendation, promulgated the education tax decree of 1993, in order to raise funds for education. This is to ensure active participation of the private sector in funding education in the country. Come to think of it, the private sector is the major user of the product of education. The decree stipulate that:

1. Education fund shall be established into which the tax money shall be paid.
2. Companies are to pay 2% of their profits, annually, as taxes and must be paid within 60 days of notification from the Federal Board of Inland Revenue.
3. A Board of Trustees shall be established for the purpose of managing and disbursing this fund, and also to monitor the Federal Inland Revenue service and ensure the collection of tax and the transfer of the fund.
4. The fund shall be disbursed in the following manner:

    a. 50% to the higher education sub-sector with universities having 50%, polytechnics 25% and colleges of education 25% of this allocation;
    b. 30% to the primary education sub-sector;
    c. 20% to the secondary education sub-sector.

5. The disbursement of this fund shall be on the basis of:

    a. Equality among the six geopolitical zones of the federation;

b. Equality among the states within a zone, and
c. Equality among the local governments within a state or the Federal Capital Territory, Abuja, respectively.

6. The fund would be used to finance development work centres, procurement of books and library facilities, purchase and maintenance of equipment.

7. The fund may sue and be sued in its corporate name in case of any mismanagement or misappropriation.

If this fund is effectively managed and disbursed, the financial crisis in the education sector shall be solved and we shall be experiencing an improved educational system with stimulating programmes. But the problem still remains management and disbursement of the fund. The curious question to ask is, "will the Board of Trustees manage and disburse this fund effectively?" The answer is left to the future.

As it has always been in this country, corruption has never allowed any worthy policy to be implemented to the letter. It has remained the major obstacle to our development in every section of the society.

It is worthy to note that these taxable companies can be categorized, so that the state and local government can be given a category within their jurisdiction. For example, category A for federal level; B — states; and C — local government.

Budgeting

A budget is a list of all goods and services for which payment may be made. Budgets are important because no matter how good an education program is, it cannot continue to operate if it has no sound fiscal foundation. Limited funds require making decisions about priorities, funding and regulatory agencies require information about monetary functions.

The expenditure level varies with the types and quality of services, with the extent of an education program and with the geographical area. These factors must be taken into consideration when preparing a budget.

A proper budget should start from the bottom to the top, that is, from the schools to the Local Education Authority (LEA) in the local government to the state, and finally to the Federal Ministry of Education. Each school budget must be treated individually to ensure its requirements are met. Budget cannot be on assumption or rough estimate; it ought to be exact in its demand.

It is an annual affair, therefore, should be done strictly for the purpose of controlling, managing and planning expenditures in the next fiscal year. Budgeting should not come from the top, otherwise, it will be based on assumption that may result to wastage. For instance, an item a school has no need for may be bought and supplied to the school, either because it has enough leftover or has no activity yet for it. Such an item definitely will lay idle and will eventually be stolen or vandalised.

A budget ensures that the operating officials adhere to policies and objectives formulated by top administration. The control aspect of the budget are necessary to discourage misappropriation of funds by enforcing accounting practice and reporting procedures. Efforts made to carry out plans and policies that have been approved efficiently and effectively is the management aspects of a budget. Objectives must be determined, alternative courses of action evaluated, and selected programmes authorised in planning a budget.

So, every school should prepare a budget to be approved at the local government level through the Local Education Authority (LEA) which must monitor and control the financial operations of the schools within its jurisdiction.

Developing a Budget

Budget usually has three components:

1. A synopsis of the programmes;
2. Specifically itemised expenditure for operating the programmes including direct cost (items that can be attributed to a particular aspect of the programme, such as personnel salaries) and indirect costs (over head items that cannot be attributed to a particular aspect of the programme, such as interest on bank loans, utility cost and advertising); and
3. Anticipated revenues and their sources, including in-kind contributions before writing the budget, the school administrator must list the programme's objectives and needs. The educational programme and the fiscal plan should be carefully related and in

writing. Although there are many ways of presenting it under the same headings as the proposed expenditures. These headings are referred to as the budget format.

Two types of format are as follows:

a. *Functional Classification*
This format put together data in terms of categories for which money must be paid, such as administration, child instruction, transportation, health services, etc., the advantage of this format is that one can readily link expenditure categories to programme purposes.

Disadvantages of this format is that it tends to be broad, raising questions as to expenditures within a classification and there is not always a distinct classification for a particular item, for example, health services may be provided within several other classification.

b. *Item Classification*
This format lists the sums allocated to specific items of the programme. The major advantage of this format is that it shows specific accountability of expenditures.

An allowance for emergencies is plausible, no matter which of the two formats is used.

There are many ways to prepare a budget with only one absolute rule of budget formulation — planned expenditure cannot exceed projected income.

The Local Property Tax

Educational programmes are very expensive. Both the scope and the quality of services are interrelated with the financial programme. One should expect positive correlation between expenditure level and quality of the educational programmes, except where money is just being wastefully spent.

Even with careful budgeting, good developmental programmes cannot operate effectively for long periods of time on insufficient funds without weakening the quality and quantity of their services, and without damaging the morale of those involved in the programmes.

As such, in addition to the Education Tax Fund at federal level, the states and local governments can operate the property tax on agreed terms in order to raise more funds to finance education. It could be named Property Tax Fund. This adds to whatever share they get from the federal level.

The property tax is calculated by applying a uniform tax rate to a tax based on the assessed valued property owned by individuals. The property tax can be classified as an *ad valorem* tax. This means that the tax is related to value (in Naira) of the property and not units (acres).

It is also a proportional tax because the tax rate is uniform, regardless of the size of the base (property). In terms of mechanics, there are four steps in the administration of a property tax. Generally, property is anything that can be owned, and real property (as opposed to personal residential property) is anything fixed or immovable in a general sense.

The property tax base also may include varying proportions of personal property, such as livestock, motor vehicles, machinery and fixtures, personal tangible and intangible property may not be taxed depending on the modality to determine "what is taxable?" It can be essentially based on real property.

The second step is to assess property for tax purposes. This is done by first determining the true value of the property: the price on an open market between a willing buyer and seller. The assessed valuation of property is some percentage of its true value.

The third step is to establish a tax rate. Exclusively, a legislative body may determine this rate.

The fourth step is to develop property tax collection procedures. Generally tax lists are prepared and bills are mailed out either semi-annually or annually.

The problems with property tax are inequalities and assessment practices that may cause property of equal value not to be assessed in the same way for tax purposes. Another problem is disparity of wealth of the various states and local governments.

States and local governments with less such taxable property may be disadvantaged when using this tax to finance their educational programmes. However, other sources of fund can assist to alleviate this situation.

On the other hand, the great advantage of property tax is that it is a predictable source of revenue and can easily be administered. It is a familiar and visible (not hidden) tax. Educational programmes can easily be planned and budgeted for with this tax system.

Educational Vouchers

This is another scheme for financing educational development of a child. Under this plan, parents are provided with a voucher to cover the cost of their child's schooling and can use it at the school of their choice. The school redeems the voucher. The average per-student/pupil expenditure in a school determines the value of the voucher.

This scheme can be used by companies, foundations and non-governmental organisations to sponsor the educational development of a child in a particular programme of their (organisation's) interest.

How to Make Education's Money Go Round

Success or failure in getting value for money from financial allocations to schools and augmenting it, can make a difference to a school's performance out of all proportion to its share in the school's total costs.

Allocating Funds

As mentioned earlier, the local government then monitors and controls the Local Education Authority to ensure financial prudence. The state likewise do same to the local government. The schools, in preparing their Local Educational Authority (LEA) in each local government, are the bottom unit which can effectively monitor and control the schools' financial operations. Estimates should try to answer questions like:

> What is the present state of provisions?
> Which areas are well poorly provided or for?
> What does each department need?
> What system of priorities should be established if the total need is greater than the resources available?

There are some strategies the school can adopt to efficiently present its need and estimate to the LEA.

The first possible approach is that which empowers the bursar to discuss with the heads of department, the needs of the coming year, matching one against another and one year against the next. He or she assesses how well last year's monies were used. If properly executed, this procedure can be quite effective because it involves some crude evaluation of cost-effectiveness. But it is time consuming, though it can be arranged in an easier way as agreed.

The second possible approach is the invitation of each department to produce estimates for the coming year, both for the ongoing expenditure and for new items. Estimates can be requested under various headings and/or in order of priority. Each department is required to justify its requests. The problem with this approach is that, the department may inflate their estimates and may not include needed items. The bursar collects and collates to send to the LEA.

The difference between this approach and the first one is that, in the first approach, the department submits list of their needs without costing them, leaving it to the bursar to estimate, whereas, the department costs their needs in the second one.

The third approach is that of assessing the percentage increase in cost in the department as made available, and then the bursar raises last year's quota for each department by that proportion. This has the advantage of being time saving and simple, but it does not make provision for special needs of priority.

Whichever strategy or approach is used, a thorough review needs to be done every few years to evolve a better and cost-effective approach.

School Financial Operations

Crediting of Income
Schools may be allowed to retain income collected for sales of materials or products from practical subjects. This may include some other extra-curricular activities like drama performances, football matches, inter-house sports, etc., which accrued income. These serve as additional income for the schools but under the watchful eyes of the LEAs.

Financing and Budgeting 195

Direct and Free Ordering
In purchasing items for educational activities, the schools may be allowed to order directly and to choose their own suppliers. The LEAs may require the schools to route requisitions via the local office, specify contract suppliers and require consent for certain large amount to be spent. This should not be a way of creating unnecessary delay.

This method helps in making sure that, each school is properly equipped and maintained to attain the educational goal.

Imprest Accounts
Imprest accounts are simply a device to give schools a sum of petty cash and replace this at intervals, debiting the allocated money. It is important to determine the amount of this account. It does allow for local purchasing of small items for immediate use instead of waiting for these small items to be supplied. The quantity may be small. Some minor maintenance can be carried out from this account. It saves time and prevents further deterioration of facilities and equipment.

School Bank Accounts
The Local Education Authority (LEA) as a monitoring organ maintains a bank account for each school, into which their respective allocation will be paid. At the request of the schools, funds adequate for their needs are released. The school's income money can also be paid into this account (current a/c), if large enough, part may be transferred to a deposit account, and the interest credited to the school. It is from this account that petty cash is drawn. Over drafts are not to be allowed, but balance can be carried forward into the next financial year. The carried forward amount should not prevent the school from getting its supposed allocation.

Over years, in the future, the carried forward amount will accumulate to an amount that can be invested by the schools. With time, the schools will become financially self-reliant, at least partially, with their investments. Donations received by school should be paid into this current account. This fund should be free from bank charges if necessary. The schools can issue out cheques to suppliers for payment of bulky or large quantity of goods supplied, but this must be with the consent of the LEA.

Some additional administration (record of bank transactions, reconciliation of statement, etc.) and extra materials must be observed. The schools should keep proper account and inventory records.

Money for educational purposes will surely go round if procedures are followed effectively. The eventual outcome is good result: gradual attainment of quality education for the mental, physical and moral development of the children in a conducive learning environment. What a better society!

REFERENCES

Adamolekun, L. 1983. *Public Administration: A Nigerian Comparative Perspective.* New York: Longman Inc.

Adaralegbe, A. 1979. "The Teaching Service." In Ladipo, A. and Gboyega, A. (eds.). *Leading Issues in Nigeria Public Service.* Ile-Ife: University of Ife Press.

Adesina, S. 1982. *Planning and Educational Development in Nigeria.* Ibadan: Board Publications Ltd.

Akabogu, G.C. 1972. "The Role Expectations of the People of the East Central State of Nigeria of the Principal of a Secondary Grammar School." An unpublished Master's Degree Thesis, University of Nigeria, Nsukka.

Cohn, E. 1975. *The Economics of Education.* Cambridge, Mass: Balinger Publishing Co.

Edem, D.A. 1987. *Introduction to Educational Administration in Nigeria.* Ibadan: Spectrum House.

Fafunwa, B. and Adaralegbe, A. 1974, *Towards Better Administration and Supervision.* Ibadan: The Conton Press.

Gorton, R.A. 1972. *Conflict, Controversy, and Crisis in School Administration and Supervision.* Lawa: W.C Brown Publishers.

Griffiths, D.C. 1962. *Organising Schools for Effective Education.* Danville, Illinois: The Interstate Printers & Publishers Inc.

Knezevich, S.J. 1975. *Administration of Public Education.* New York: Harper & Row Publishers.

Morgan, J.E. 1973. *Principles of Administration and Supervisory Management.* Englewood Cliffs, N.J.: Prentice Hall Inc.

Mort, P.R. 1980. *Public School Finance: Its Background, Structure and Operation.* London: McGraw-Hill Book Company Inc.

Nwankwo, J.I. 1982. *Educational Administration: Theory and Practice.* New Delhi: Vikas Publishing House.

Olubadewo, S.O. 1992. *Fundamentals of Educational Administration and Planning.* Ilesa: Jola Publishing Ltd.

Ozigi, A.O. 1978. *A Handbook on School Administration and Management.* London: Macmillan Educational Ltd.

Reddin, W.J. 1970. *Managerial Effectiveness.* New York: McGraw-Hill.

Sergiovanni, S. 1971. *Emerging Patterns of Supervision: Human Perspectives.* New York: McGraw-Hill.

Ukeje, B.O. Akabogu, G.C. and Ndu, A. 1992. *Educational Administration.* Enugu: Fourth Dimension Publishers.

Wiles, K. and Lovell, A. 1975. *Supervision for Better Schools.* Englewood Cliffs, N.J.: Prentice Hall Inc.

Wiles, K. 1976, *Supervision for Better Schools.* Englewood Cliffs, N.J.: Prentice Hall Inc.

Chapter Ten

WHAT SORT OF FUTURE?

Government Actions
Let's take a brief look at some of the deliberate, purposeful and well-intentioned programmes, policies, laws and treaties put in place by the Federal Government over the years, for the development, welfare and protection of the child in Nigeria.

Ratification of the Convention
In March 1991, Nigeria ratified the convention on the rights of the child. Before this ratification, some national programmes and policies that were supportive of issues and concerns relating to the development and welfare of the child were already pursued. Most notable existing national policies concerning the rights of the child are, National Policy on Health establishment in 1991, National Policy on Population of 1988, National Policy on Education of 1981 and the Social Development Policy for Nigeria established in 1989.

The Better Life Programme, which was inaugurated in 1987 and formalised by Decree 42 of 1992, was another government programme aimed at promoting maternal and child care at the grassroots.

The Federal Government took some measures that led to the ratification of the convention, and these include the following:
1. In September 1990, the Federal Ministry of Culture and Social Welfare organised a national seminar on the Nigerian child to sensitise the general public on the importance of the child.

2. In the same September 1990, a government delegate represented Nigeria at the World Summit for Children.

3. In February 1991, the Federal Ministry of Culture and Social Welfare established a National Child Welfare Committee to formulate a national framework for implementing the goals of the World Summit for Children.

4. In March 1991, the government established a trust fund for the Nigerian child to help develop the talents of children through arts and cultural activities. It also raised funds for the execution of programmes and projects designed for child welfare services especially for disabled children.

These are to give support to the advancement of child survival in Nigeria. The Federal Government went on to review and harmonise laws and policies relating to women and children after a national conference on women and children was held in October 1989. This review was made to be in harmony with the provisions of the convention.

Legislation
The following are laws that protect the child in Nigeria:

1. The Nigeria Labour Act of 1990 protects children from exploitation and abuse.
2. Children and Young Persons Law, 1958.
3. Cinematography Act of 1990 protects children from exposure to indecent and obscene materials, publication and films.
4. Criminal law, which prohibits the sale and trafficking of children.
5. Tobacco and alcohol advertisement decrees forbid the use of children in the advertisement of cigarette and alcoholic beverages.
6. In 1993, a draft of children's decree, which took into account the convention on the rights of the child, the OAU Charter on the Right and Welfare of the Child and the Beijing rules was produced and signed into law.

Programmes for Implementation of the Convention

Various mechanisms were set up to co-ordinate policies and monitor the implementation of the convention by sensitising the public.

In August 1991, Mass Mobilisation for Social Justice, Self-Reliance and Economic Recovery (MAMSER) and the African Network for the Prevention and Protection Against Child Abuse and Neglect in Nigeria (ANPPCAN), jointly organised a workshop on the rights of the child in Nigeria.

The Federal Ministry of Culture and Social Welfare organised a national seminar in March 1992, to sensitise the media executives on the implementation of the rights of the child. This led to the signing of a statement of commitment by the representative of media institutions and allied professions to promote the convention and the OAU Charter on the rights and welfare of the child. They are to monitor and report any observation and abuse of children's rights in the society.

The National Commission for Women in 1989, took over the welfare services of the child from the Ministry of Health and Social Services, thereby, creating a functional child welfare department in 1991. The Commission was extended to the states and the local governments.

A National Committee on Women and Children was also set up in 1991 to review all laws concerning the welfare of children and women.

In March 1993, a National Working Committee on Child Welfare was inaugurated by the National Commission for Women, charged with the responsibility of coming up with strategies for effective delivery of child development services in Nigeria and for promoting collaboration among relevant ministries and organisations on the development and protection of the child.

The Federal Government in October 1994 inaugurated a National Child Rights Implementation Committee, with the purpose of:

1. Initiating actions that would ensure the popularization of the UN Convention on the Rights of the Child and the OAU Charter on the Rights and Welfare of the Child.

2. Continuous review of the state of implementation of these rights in Nigeria.

3. Developing and recommending to government specific programmes and projects that will improve the status of the Nigerian child.

4. Instituting an appropriate mechanism that will enable Nigeria monitor and evaluate the implementation of the provisions of the convention.
5. Collecting and collating data on the implementation of the child rights treaties.
6. Preparing and submitting periodic reports on the state of implementation to the Federal Government.

This committee has membership which include relevant federal ministries, non-governmental organisations, academic institutions, the media, child-care experts, and UN agencies as observers.

Creating Public Awareness
To further broaden the support for the development and welfare of the child and to advance and implement the rights of the child, some other programme mechanisms exist to create awareness on issues relating to the child in Nigeria, such as:

1. The First Lady's concert for the Nigerian Children's Trust Fund, which is to raise funds for children's talents enhancing programmes and welfare services on annual event.
2. The Family Support Programme, which resulted from the 1994 declaration by the United Nations of the International Year of the Family (IYF) is committed to organising programmes that will increase children participation in their socio-educational development.
3. The June 16th Day of African Child annual event in line with the OAU resolution of creating a positive change for children throughout the continent. This is also in line with the World Summit for Children; the Dakar consensus. This is used to create public awareness on the right of the child and their implementation.
4. The National Children's and Youth Day celebration on May 27 yearly. The day also promotes children's competitions, rallies, art and toy development, dialogues with government officials and policy makers, and other educational stimulating programmes.
5. National children's holiday camp designed to promote national unity,

understanding and interaction among Nigerian children and educate them on their rights.

The Media Role

To complement these government efforts, the mass media have continued to enlighten the public on the importance of implementing the rights of the child as contained in the convention. They have come up with radio and television programmes for the children, and even children magazines are being published.

The Non-Governmental Organisation (NGO)

The non-governmental organisations (NGO) are not left out in their support to government efforts. They have established day care centres, running orphanages, setting up counselling centres, research and data collection, and enlightenment campaign on various issues relating to the welfare of the child in Nigeria. Such NGO as the Nigerian chapter of African Network for the Prevention and Protection of Child Abuse and Neglect in Nigeria (ANPPCAN) has established in Nigeria, regional monitoring centres on child rights violation.

Education: Policy and Programmes

Coming to education, which is one of the rights of the child in the convention, the Federal Government has formulated policy and carried out programmes that are to enhance the development and education of the child both socially and culturally.

The National Policy on Education spells out the need for children from 6-12 years to undergo six years of primary education and three years of junior secondary education. The aim is to provide basic education of functional literacy in numeracy skills and effective communication skills at primary level.

The Junior Secondary Education is aimed at enabling children to acquire a broad based education in the development of mind, in understanding the world around and the appropriate skills, abilities and competence both mentally and physically to live and contribute to the development of the society.

The Science and Technology Policy makes possible science education at all levels to enable children have early contact with the concepts of science, and materials related to science and technology before attaining primary school age. It also ensures a sound science foundation during the first six years of the 6-3-3-4 educational structures through entrenchment of science teaching in the primary school curriculum.

The policy provision is to be implemented at the same time at the federal, state, and local government levels.

Early Childhood Education

The Federal Government in collaboration with relevant donor agencies, such as UNICEF, UNESCO and educational institutions also launched early childhood education programme, day care centres were to be established in urban and rural areas. The programme orientation is informal, low-cost community based and targeted at families with low income.

Curriculum guidelines for early childhood education were developed and monitoring mechanism put in place for supervising and inspecting nursery schools in order to ensure compliance to set standards.

The National Primary Education Commission was set up to avert the deteriorating and possible collapse of primary education in Nigeria. Budgeting allocation was provided for development of facilities, equipment and personnel management.

Aid

A World Bank assisted Primary Education Project for six years (1991-1996) was expected to implement the following major schemes:

1. Training of about 400,000 education personnel for primary schools.
2. Provision of textbooks in five basic subjects and creation of a permanent text book fund.
3. Action research, especially in critical areas such as national assessment of achievements and optional use of local environment.
4. Data/information management with emphasis on primary education.

Free Basic Education

Free and compulsory basic education for nine years, covering primary and junior secondary education, for all children has been put in place by the Federal Government. The aims of this are:

1. To ensure that all children in the age bracket of six years are enrolled in primary schools and complete their education.
2. To ensure a complete transition from primary school to junior secondary schools.
3. To reduce illiteracy rate and dropout syndrome and to increase their number of years in school.
4. To develop their creative skills at the junior secondary school level where technical and vocational education is emphasised.
5. To ensure that girl-child education is emphasised and made possible.

Nomadic Education
As a resolve to educate every Nigerian child, the government established a National Commission for Nomadic Education to meet educational needs of the children of nomads and migrant fishermen. Budgetary allocation was made to fund the training of teachers and provision of equipment to implement the programme.

Research studies are being carried out for the take-off of "schools in boats" programme for children of fishermen in the reverine areas of the country.

The liberalisation of the establishment of special schools by the Federal Government is aimed at providing education for the physically and mentally handicapped and gifted children. This is to enable private establishment of such schools.

Leisure and Cultural Activities for Education
In Article XII of the African Charter on the Rights and Welfare of the Child, in conformity with the UN convention, the child should engage in leisure related educational activities. Pre-primary and primary school curriculum in Nigeria has been made to contain these leisure activities. Such activities include art and crafts, gardening, fishing and games, and interstate exchange programme. Children's concerts, drama and debates are regular features on national network radio and television programmes.

In recognition of the needs for children to be culturally educated, and the fact that Nigeria is a culturally diverse country, the Federal Government developed a cultural policy on education, which stipulates culturally relevant school activities for children. The learning of local crafts and traditional cooking are now part of the curriculum. The use of the mother tongue for teaching and learning is also encouraged in schools.

Based on the cultural policy on education, the following activities are articulated to foster the cultural education and training of children:

1. Development of educational activities for children and youths in Nigerian museums.
2. Documentation and development into pamphlets the Nigerian folklore resources.
3. Cultural exhibitions and competitions between primary and secondary school children at zonal and national levels to hold annually.
4. Mandatory basic education in the mother tongue during pre-primary school and the first three years of primary education. At junior and senior secondary level, students are required to study one Nigerian language apart from their mother tongue.

Defects in the System
Scanning through various government actions as summarised earlier in this chapter, one will agree they are commendable and laudable. A non-Nigerian who avails himself of this information will be impressed, and believe that the Nigerian children are being given deserved attention and proper care by the government and the society.

The picture in the vision of the mind of such a person is one of protected children, well-equipped educational system, and cultured children. An impressive ideal situation — very much expected.

But is that what we have or almost what we have on the ground? Unfortunately, what is on the ground is not proportional to government effort, financially and otherwise. If this is true, which of course it is, the curious question any concerned person will ask is, "what is wrong?" Or simply, "why?" Other intriguing questions will be, "are we doing it wrongly?" "Why are we not doing it right?" "What is causing our failure?" The questions are endless.

Examine these factors:

Discrimination
Indeed, a lot of things are done wrongly and on the surface too. In the first place, these programmes on the rights of the child, education in particular, ought to be grass roots programmes in order to affect the life of every child in the country.

But are they? No! When you talk of television and radio programmes for children such as debate, concert, drama, magazine publication for children, field trips, recreational activities, etc. you are talking of urbanised programmes, yet it narrows down to involve mostly children of the affluent in the society. Rich parents make sure their children are the beneficiaries of these programmes and are always dominating. Rarely do you have children from poor homes participating, if any, then it is sheer luck. These "elite" children may probably account for 1% of children population in Nigeria, what happens to the rest 99% of the children's population?

The implementation of these educational programmes starts and ends with these "elite" children. And it is assumed and accepted that the implementation is going on well; the children are getting what they deserve is always the claim.

Popular names and schools are being used as samples for implementing educational policies and programmes. Truly these schools are well equipped with teaching and learning materials with qualified teachers. The children who attend such schools are selected and "classified" children. Their parents' purse must be of considerable size, otherwise, they have no business being there.

These schools are few but they get all the attention and support from the government. They are called Unity Schools or Federal Government Colleges. They are not seen as public schools, the unpopular schools are the public schools; the dumping ground for children of low-income parents. The unpopular schools are not worthy of being samples for implementation; they are not worthy of participating in radio and television education programmes.

The worst hit are schools in the rural areas. Those are forgotten establishments. The rural children should remain "rural", they dare not think of exposure. Poor children, what can they do about it? What a hopeless and helpless situation! How many of the rural schools go on excursions? How many are featured in media programmes? How many are sent on holiday camping? Perhaps, they do not need it. Yet these programmes are claimed to be for the educational development of all the children in Nigeria. Who then really cares?

Some private schools are beginning to enjoy the patronage of the "high and mighty" in the society whose children now attend some of these schools. These are "exclusive" private schools and are indirectly financially supported, after all, their proprietors are among the "high and mighty" and their participation in government are undoubted. Special children in special schools are treated specially so to speak.

There is nothing wrong with this set up in a given society, what is wrong is the very wide gap that exists between the rich and the poor in this country. The implication of this practice is discrimination, that is, the majority of talented children are undiscovered and wasted away.

Non-grass roots Implementation
This discriminatory practice has cut deep to the extent that these government educational policies and programmes are not implemented in the grass roots. This is simply because those who are saddled with the responsibility of implementation are not the right people. Consequently, they take the process of implementation to the wrong quarters or places.

The employed personnel charged with the responsibilities of implementing the policies are the same officials in the ministries and people in other high positions, who have no time and are not ready to get down to the grass roots to ensure implementation. These are parents of the "elite" children in exclusive schools, which are used as samples for implementation only to claim a wide spread success of the policy and programmes. That is to say, they implement the programmes on their children alone.

Take for instance, the Better Life Programme, later the Family Support Programme, the Child Welfare Services, the Rights of the Child programmes, etc., which of these has benefited the children at the grass roots where the bulk of the children in Nigeria belong? Grass roots simply implies the poor masses in the society no matter where they reside.

The teachers and parents at the grass roots, who have close

communication with 99% of the Nigerian children, whose actions in one way or the other affect the children, are excluded from the core personnel responsible for implementing policies and programmes relating to children.

What has the man in the office got to do with children in the street? Who are close to the children if not teachers and parents? Who are to implement the rights of the child if not teachers and parents?

The government has not actively involved teachers and parents in implementing the policy and programmes formulated. The government simply handed down instructions to these people without "tools" to work with.

In the years gone by, when missions established, ran and financed schools, teachers were responsible for implementing all educational programmes and policy as well as ensure discipline in the children. They were so trained and equipped in such a way that instructions effectively imparted to them were executed to the letter. Children were occupied with educational activities, practically and theoretically in schools. They were being exposed to various activities that developed their creative abilities. Of course, teachers and staff were being paid promptly, and the welfare of the children were of paramount interest to the missionaries and the teachers.

There was discipline among the children, between the teachers and children, and between the teachers and the proprietors. Teachers had good relationship with parents which fostered the children's learning. Infrastructures and instructional materials were adequately made available. Conferences were held with teachers to enlighten them on new policy or programmes for the children. No matter where the headquarters of the missions were, schools established by them were being properly run and funded. Learning was learning in the true sense, but that was then.

Though parents paid school fees and other levies if necessary, they were happy because their children always came out proving they had actually schooled. They saw the worth of the fees paid. The missions, in the form of training their children on scholarship, encouraged even some parents who could not afford the fees. Many of the politicians, educationists, etc., in the society today are beneficiaries of this gesture of the missions. Learning was spread out to include all willing and ready children. Those children who failed go to school did as a result of traditional and cultural constraints.

Today, government has stepped in (a welcomed development) to take education to the doorstep of every family, this is a good idea. But what is happening? The traditional responsibilities of the teachers are being subverted and those in the office are the implementors. They are members of the implementation committee, members of trust funds, members of commissions and so on.

Are these grass roots people? Any thing short of involving the grass roots people (parents and teachers) is a superficial implementation bound to fail.

Financial Misappropriation

A critical look at government expenditure on implementing policy and programmes relating to children, especially in education, will reveal an astonishing and outrageous amount in millions and billions of Naira, which practically has created no impact whatsoever to the welfare, development and protection of the children in this country, international agencies such as UNESCO, UNICEF, WHO and World Bank have provided financial and material aids to programmes that are for the welfare and development of the children. Even non-governmental organisations are making their contributions. Yet it appears as if nothing is being done. Where are these funds going?

Some people may want to put up an argument that population is growing fast. Quite true, but those millions or billions of Naira being wasted in one way or the other, if properly channelled, could create a gradual impact that will build up over a period of time. The problem is, funds are being misappropriated — corruption.

For instance, millions or billions of Naira are being squandered in organising seminars, conferences and workshops on issues affecting children and women in Nigeria. Huge hotel bills are paid, pamphlets are printed and souvenirs are made for attendees, there is usually wining and dining, extensive publicity and cosy environments for the attendees who are the "who is who" in our society, the venues are always out of the reach of the grass roots people; the home front of majority of their children.

These attendees are mostly people who do not come in contact with children in the street; whose children are being provided with the best in life; made individuals who lacked virtually nothing. At the end of the day, the intellectual theories would have been said, very easy, but the practical aspect remains the hardest part of it all, that is something no attendee has time for. This wasted money would have had a better impact on the children if it was sincerely and practically appropriated for the needs of the children.

Various commissions and committees are regular features in government circles which look into issues relating to one problem or the other on programmes and policies. Members are constituted and huge amount voted for their take-off and maintenance. The same old faces, increasing and multiplying financially, reserving for their privileged children the advantages of government policies. Finally, nothing concrete comes out of them: we are still in the dark tunnel.

Nigerian "elite" are very good in solving problems only intellectually. It is easy, it is comfortable and convenient. But it is tedious and humiliating when it comes to practically solving the problems; an attitude that has made implementation difficult at all levels for all policies and programmes.

It is quite easy to lay defensive claim to save face, that something substantial and tangible has been achieved; that lives of the children have improved as compared to the past; and a long list of achievements rehearsed.

If anything has been achieved, if the lives of most Nigerian children have improved, if the Nigerian children are adequately protected against social aggression, then, why are there still the problems of more girls in prostitution and more children engaged in child labour, cultism and drug addiction? Why are children still learning under the trees, in dilapidated buildings and filthy environment called schools? How many of the nomadic children are in the university today after many years nomadic education has been introduced and funded heavily? Are their lives truly touched? Where are the funds going? The problems are still there, increasing instead.

Peeping into the Future

What sort of future do we want for the Nigerian children, which incidentally, is the future of Nigeria? Do we continue in our ineffective and inadequate approach to implementation? There is need for a change in approach if we really want a better future for the children, the eventual leaders of future Nigeria.

Education will undergo more fundamental changes in the next twenty years this new millennium than in the last hundred years. This is as a result of the "jet" transition from Industrial Revolution Age to Information Revolution Age. The new educational technology will soon burst upon us: home learning will be facilitated, and individual learning transformed. At the same time, new forces in the economy and in the society will make new educational demands. Can the schools of one era serve another era unaltered?

Our schools have not yet passed through the industrial revolution, for typical school classroom of the 1960s is still being used today. The impact of the dawn of a technological transformation — audio-visual aids, programmed learning, educational television — in education is yet to be felt in our educational system.

We need to peer ahead to identify likely trends and assess their financial implications. Unless we can think ahead, develop new approaches and loosen constraints, we shall find ourselves trying to finance a new system with the policies and procedures of the old system.

Already, some of the main features of the information revolution are becoming apparent. Information itself is becoming the most important factor of production above land, labour or capital. It is expanding exponentially and yet is increasingly accessible. In a few years, it will be a common place for a person in his own home to command a pool of knowledge far greater than it can be done today. Information will be instantly available and transferable worldwide.

The trend for activities to be home-centred will increase, such as shopping, private banking, commercial transactions and other aspects of life activities. These are challenges ahead for our educational system.

The Schools of the Future

Schools will continue to provide substantial education on a teacher and class basis. This will be important in the primary and junior secondary levels, with emphasis on basic skills and on socialisation.

Individualised learning systems, both inside and outside schools will increase, and learning will be more individual centred. The learner may select his own programmes.

The schools will act as a learning centre for the community, with teachers as advisers, technical assistants, sophisticated resources and equipment providing guidance and feedback services. They will also serve as a social centre for learners because of the leisure and recreational facilities available. It is likely that a high proportion of the school children will be adolescents and adults.

Changes in the Future School Curriculum

1. Learning skills and attitude are the most important task which schools which have to instil in young children; a general curiosity and a pleasure in learning. The worst damage that could be done to young children would be for their schooling to leave them with no desire or capacity for learning. More positively, there is need for a deliberate emphasis on developing study skills, particularly those related to independent learning which is likely to play a major part in the schemes of recurrent and continuing education.
2. Basic communication skills will be even more important — orally, numeracy, graphical communication.
3. Physical skills in design, crafts and technology, acts and physical education, both as a base for leisure activities and for vocational skills.
4. New skills will be needed relating to information technology — computing.
5. Social education — development of social skills and personal qualities.
6. Transmission of our cultural, historical and religious heritage.
7. Development of moral and political understanding and values.
8. Support for children with personal and family problems.
9. Career guidance and career education.

The curriculum must change in response to the needs of the information revolution, and this will also necessitate similar series of changes in learning and teaching methods. The schools will have to be reorganised to meet the challenges. This definitely will have financial implication, for school cost will increase. The introduction of a large amount of electronic technology or equipment into schools will require non-teaching technicians' cost and the cost of equipment provision and maintenance. Teachers' salaries will increase and clerical support will be needed.

Financing the Future Schools

The schools of the information revolution will be more expensive to run, therefore such changes can only be financed in one of the following ways:

1. The Federal Government reversing the current trend and increasing education's share of the national income.
2. The introduction of educational charges and fees of various kinds accordingly. That is, the government could agree that a defined general education should be free, but that items additional to that should be paid for. In other words, government could finance a certain amount of fringe items as well as the core items and leave a smaller range of additional items for parents to pay. The free area has to be properly defined. This would then leave freedom for individuals to pay for topping up items.
3. Sales of services offered to the schools, members of the community and even school children; a sort of business centre. School income can be generated from some business activities engaged by the schools without disrupting educational activities. The Federal Government accepting the financial implications of these radical changes in educational conditions can create more flexible regulations and policies to allow for adjustment. This would allow the additional finance needed for the likely changes to be funded or sourced from within the schools without hindering educational programmes.

Financial Control and Monitor

With computerised information systems, it will be much easier for the Federal or state government to establish a tighter control and monitor over local authorities, and for local authorities to establish similar control on schools with constant watchfulness for aberration from the norm.

Another important aspect is that, due to increased centralisation and bureaucratisation of our educational system, there has been decline in the performance records of schools in recent years. This has caused so much disaffection and there is a need for steps to be taken towards decentralising educational decision-making, thereby providing grass roots participation in the decision-making process. It will also provide for greater local discretion in the use of financial resources made available for the schools. It is then easier for the schools to control their own budget in line with scarce financial resources.

New Approaches to Implementation of Policy and Programmes

Grass roots

The implementation of policy and programmes should be a two way flow of information, that is, from the top to the bottom and from the bottom back to the top. This implies that the relevant ministries, commissions and committees at federal level responsible for implementing policy and programmes on education, including others relating to the development and welfare of children, should communicate information on these directly to the parents and teachers at the grass roots, who are to educate the children and create impact in their lives.

The parents and teachers on their own part, through observation and participation, are able to send feedback information to the appropriate ministry, commission or committee for review, adjustment or reinforcement.

This direct communication from the federal level to the grass roots (parents and teachers) should be made to pass through the Local Education Authority in each local government area. The LEA then oversees the activities of the Parents-Teachers Association (PTA) in respect of the implementation.

It is therefore plausible that the federal level deals directly with the local government, with the responsibility resting on the Local Education Authority to organise seminars, workshops and conferences in the various communities within its jurisdiction in order to enlighten parents, teachers, and community leaders on the programmes and policy to be implemented.

The local government should be equipped with all necessary logistics for effectiveness. This also should be allocated to the local government, directly bypassing the state government to avoid delay in take-off of activities. Nevertheless, the federal level must carry along state representatives who act as a monitoring unit to the activity of the Local Government Authority (LEA) in respect of the set goal.

In organising the seminars, workshops or conferences, the Local Education Authority must have federal and state representatives as guest speakers, for clarity and emphasis, present in the occasion. Parents-Teachers-Students seminars, conferences or workshops holding in schools are very essential and necessary.

This grass roots enlightenment in all aspects will create a far reaching effect on the development and welfare of the children than organising seminars, workshops and conferences at the federal level, thereby making them exclusive. Take the campaign, therefore, to the grass roots — Local Government Areas (L.G.As).

Non-discrimination on Educational Activities

We should imbibe a new attitude and approach to implementing our educational policy and programmes, and the distribution of infrastructures, equipment and materials for teaching and learning in schools.

As alluded earlier, the Local Education Authority has a lot to put in for effective implementation at the grass roots. This effort should be seen in areas as follows:

1. Schools must have schedules of varieties of recreational and cultural activities, which must be exposed through intra and inter-school competitions. Every school in the LEA jurisdiction is made compulsory to participate in all the educational activities.
2. Schools in rural areas should be given media exposition in these activities. Such exposure will motivate the children to want to participate and excel. It arouses interest and captures the child's attention to learning.
3. To develop and extend keen competitions among schools within and without; the Local Education Authorities should interact with the aim of facilitating such programmes.
4. Infrastructures and facilities must be put in place for these activities.
5. The LEA should have or cultivate a cordial working relationship with Parent-Teachers' Association to work out ways of implementing programmes and policy for maximum benefit of the children.
6. Schools in the rural areas should be involved in national competitions alongside those in the urban areas according to the results from the various LEA Competitions at the local government level.

It is only through compulsory participation of all schools in all the local government areas, in all educational programmes, would there be an effective and even implementation of policy on education. In this circumstance, can failure or success of a policy be ascertained?

Financial Appropriation and Accountability

The Federal Government allocating educational funds directly to the Local Education Authority bank account, through the local government, will eliminate misappropriation of funds by either state or local government. For record and check purposes, the state and local governments should be furnished with financial information on such allocation.

With a computerised financial system in the LEA, the financial transactions of the LEA are easily accessible for audition. And because the LEA is a small operating unit, its accounts will not be ambiguous and complicated for auditing by state auditors. Another major advantage is the practice of some high degree of transparency and accountability in that, a school in the district of the LEA cannot acknowledge receipt of a fund not disbursed to it by the LEA for any project or activity.

In like manner, as the schools operate their respective bank accounts, the LEA disburse funds directly into the schools' accounts to run the school budget for the year. The school too is a small operating unit whose accounts can be easily audited by local government auditors.

This approach, if effectively outlined and implemented, will ensure a better financial appropriation and accountability. Surely, this will create a uniformed, conducive learning environment in all our schools. The bureaucratic bottleneck at either state or local government level is removed, and a free flow of funds and actualisation of goals are achieved.

The Federal Government knows whom to hold responsible for any financial failure — mismanagement and misappropriation — in a particular local government, obviously, the Local Education Authority.

Suggestions on School Finances

There is absolute need for schools to compliment the Federal Government financial allocation to them if the right type of education for the children is to be achieved. Provision of infrastructures, equipment and material for schools is one thing, maintaining and remodelling is another thing. Of the two aspects, maintaining and remodelling are very important, otherwise, continuous deterioration will bring about a collapse. Quick minor repairs are necessary to avert expanded damages, and this school can do without having to apply for high level approval and fund which delays.

The financial burden may be too heavy at times for the government to bear alone, even with the help of some other organisations. Education is the biggest industry and therefore the most capital intensive, being the foundation of all forms of development in human endeavours.

Therefore, the idea of schools trying to generate funds for expenditures that need quick attention is not bad at all.

A quick warning; this is not a part of government allocation, but a complementary effort and should not be totally relied upon by the government as the major means of financing schools.

Sources

The sources of generating these schools funds could be from products of practical lessons in schools such as farming (poultry, animal, crop, fishery), art and crafts (paintings, carvings, moulding and sculpturing), and domestic science (cooking, baking, knitting and sewing). In technical schools, carpentry products, mechanical and electrical services can generate funds for the schools.

There is nothing wrong with young school children engaging in these creative activities that aid in exposing their respective talent, giving them practical lessons in various fields of life endeavours.

At various times, exhibition or fair is organised by the schools and held in the schools for these products of the handiwork of the children. Parents and other dignitaries in the communities are invited to come and purchase these. Prizes are awarded to the pupil/group of pupils or student/group of students, as the case may be, whose works are being exhibited to encourage others and stimulate their appetite for participation and learning.

Another viable source is investment opportunities, which the government must create by passing legislature that will enable schools to participate in capital investments to make extra money with whatever funds they have. If churches like Catholic and Baptist can buy stock/shares to build up their internal finance, then let us try the experiment with the schools up to the universities, polytechnics and colleges of education levels. The long-term benefit is that, the schools in the future may become adequately financed, expanded and developed to an enviable standard.

Such scheme as the Sinking Fund Scheme could be employed for this investment strategy, using fund available in the Education Tax Fund.

The Federal Government can fund certain school capital projects, improving facilities like recreational facilities, which can serve the community as resource centres with the schools charging fees for such services. The Sinking Fund and Amortisation Loan Scheme can play a profitable role in this type of investment projects.

The Benefits of Practical Lessons in Schools

Some years ago, school children were actively engaged in practical lessons in agricultural and domestic sciences and manual arts. But such practice gradually died off, because of short-sightedness in seeing the benefits of these in the lives of the children and the schools in the future.

There was no serious emphasis on this practice on the part of education authorities and, therefore, it could not be funded and expanded for the actual benefits to be realised in the long run.

The truth is, this is a developmental programme with a whole lot of benefits, both to the children and the schools at all levels of our educational chain. Let us examine some of the benefits that are immense in scope and nature.

Products from these practical lessons, as earlier highlighted, when sold outside the school community through whatever methods adopted, are able to accrue some incomes to the schools. If expanded, the incomes increase.

At the secondary and tertiary levels, the products not only provide incomes, but also products yielding from poultry, animal, crop and fishery farming. Cooking and baking can as well be used to feed boarding students while the excesses are sold. This will surely alleviate the financial burden of such students on their parents and government as well.

The schools, especially the tertiary institutions running medium or large-scale farms in its category according to departments, will indeed feed the student and the nation as a whole. What do you expect from our would-be professionals in these fields if not the best, for practice brings perfection.

The third and fourth year students in the tertiary institutions should be seriously and actively involved in these practical lessons, as they prepare them through practical experience to know and to face the challenges ahead.

Those departments of non-edible products such as electrical/ electronics, mechanical, civil and chemical engineering, and other fields of science and technology can contribute in their respective ways to save the schools and government some money. For instance, maintenance of school computers, building, vehicles, electrical appliances, campus roads, and the production of farm chemicals to help the school farms would go a long way.

There are many ways to put the students into use within the school community without oppressing or enslaving them. These practical lessons must not be an avenue for punishment and exploitation, but a learning process that is motivating and pleasurable. The aim of this idea or programme is to impart the ethics of professionalism in the students in their various fields.

For example, a situation where outside services are sought to repair broken down computers where there are computer engineering students, who in one or two years are going to be practising this profession in the society are available, is unacceptable and complete fund wasting. What have the students learned through the years in school? Technical school students are not left out of this.

Involving young school children and youths in these practical activities according to individual interest and talent not only excite them, but also keeps their minds busy in something very useful and developmental, at the same time, maintaining a conducive teaching and learning environment that is stimulating.

This moulds their behaviour in the right shape and form required of a dedicative, patriotic person. It is another form of discipline. This is the most profound benefit of practical lessons in schools, their attentions are constantly placed on learning and taken away from those social vices they mostly find themselves engaged in these days. "An idle mind", it is said, "is the devil's workshop".

"Experience is the best teacher", so goes a saying. Truly, if a child experiences something, the knowledge of that experience sticks in his memory for a long time and could easily be retrieved when required.

This means he knows it and can make use of it anytime, any day. Such assurance build self-confidence in that individual with which a problem can be handled convincingly.

Another quality that unfolds in the course of this is self-reliance, which means he is able to stand on his feet at any point in time to pilot his life. In other words, he can be independent if he so desires. It is just another benefit. If one experiences he knows and he knows, first hand.

Practical lessons provide an excellent opportunity for gifted children who may be more practical by nature than theoretical. In so doing, their talents are enhanced, their curiosity aroused and their interests held spellbound, such that, they are able to toil on their innate ideas, who knows, maybe invent or discover something of use to the society.

Consequently, the goal of our science and technology policy is achieved, for it is mostly from these gifted children that something extraordinary can happen. It is too motivating.

These professed new approaches to both implementations of policy, programmes and school finances are to co-ordinate the efforts of educators, teachers, parents, the society and pupils/students to actualise government efforts to bring education to the grass roots in Nigeria.

The Sinking Fund and Amortisation Loan Scheme

The Education Tax Fund Approach

1. Education tax fund seeks among other things the mobilisation of capital for the enhancement and development of Nigerian schools, for rehabilitation, remodelling and maintenance of these developed schools.
2. The mobilisation of capital (with indices from financial resources principally required from the education tax funds) for investment purpose and other forms of aid/grant/technical assistance is an extreme uphill task considering the volatility of the body polity and ecohomic downgraded stature of schools marred over three decades by political instability, incoherent fiscal policies, incessant interference in governance by internal forces, etc. This gloomy indicators make it extremely difficult for confidence coefficient to be established

for banks to risk any fiscal injection of fund (to these schools) by way of lending for development purposes.

3. The board of trustee of Education Tax Fund as the financial and fiscal control nerve centre of the programme (by and through its management directorate board), has the audacious responsibility of liaising with the 10 funding affiliate banks (prime accredited financial institutions), both within the local government and state in mobilizing the interest acquired as investment capital on a low interest rate with limitation placed, on its tenured-security and a freeze on its interest index during the placement tenure to enable the programme fully implement the developmental contents of its fiscal and functional elective as cited in (I) above.

4. BOT/ETF has functional linkages with some concern groups in the country and international R & D institutions, and can place a trust account (aid, and grant fund) for running of its investment funds.

The application of these dates is in the designing of techniques to enhance and develop adaptive technology for our schools. The expendable man-hours required for consulting directorates to effect these objectives are financially and professionally traumatic.

How the Scheme Works

1. Proponent (schools) will on application ask to borrow ₦10,000,000 from ETF.
2. ₦5,000,000 will be for the project as per the schools' financing and investment plans; this is disbursed directly to proponent's (the school) bankers.
3. ₦5,000,000 will be set aside in an investment account in the name of the proponent. This account is called the sinking fund, for the premier funding cycle of the programmes. This account is used in part to purchase these prime collateral instruments for the guarantee index factor of the loan.
4. The tenure on all the programmes of sinking fund and amortisation loan scheme to schools is 3 years + 1 day. During this period, proponent makes interest payments only on the principal amount borrowed. (₦5,000,000) no principal payment are made.

5. With the diverse range of investment models to which the sinking fund is applied, interest earnings are periodically recorded and saved to augment payment on the interest payments as per the drawn-up interest repayment schedules of the loan.
6. After 3 years + 1 day loan duration, the sinking fund portion would have grown to become ₦5,000,000.
7. The size of the sinking fund is governed by the fluctuation of the money market and determined by the prevailing interest rate at the time of closing. It is managed in full by the programme within the preview of the fund management agreement which would have been enacted and entered into force prior to funding.
8. As soon as commitment to fund is given effect, the loans review council in conjunction with the project funding committee at the BOT/ETF will communicate with the proponent (school), a letter providing the latter with a letter of commitment to issue prime collateral instruments to cover the loan in particular, and assurance for repayment of principal thereof.

Vision 2010 on Education
It is noteworthy to allude here to the report of some visionary Nigerians, who were tasked to peer into the future to see the likely picture of our educational system and ascertain how to attain the much desired goal in effectively educating the Nigerian children and youths.

Their recommended plan and actions, if honestly and effectively implemented alongside those solutions, recommendations, suggestions, and new approaches discussed in the previous chapters of this book, will result to building a more viable, sustainable, solid foundation for education to match the challenges of the future.

The report is commendable. And for information purpose, the following are the Action Plan on Education as stipulated in the main report of the Vision 2010 Committee of 1997:
1. Provide special schools for the physically and mentally handicapped and abandoned children. Provide for the treatment and upkeep of lunatics.
2. Expand and improve the quality of science, engineering and technology education/training at the vocational, secondary and tertiary levels.

3. Encourage French as a second language in our education curriculum.
4. Commence the spending of the accumulated revenue from the education tax.
5. Encourage private sector to fund independent research institutes in universities.
6. Inaugurate a Teachers' Registration Council to support and promote professionalism, continuing education and high standards.
7. Create more schools for girls in science and technology and encourage NGOs to stimulate interest in scientific courses for women.
8. Make compulsory and free, primary and secondary education by year 2003 and 2009 respectively, for all Nigerian children between the ages of 6 and 18 years.
9. Improve the quality of the educational management in various universities.
10. Amend the draft constitution to delineate responsibilities for education funding as follows:
    a. Funding of primary education should be the responsibility of the local government;
    b. Funding of secondary education should be the responsibility of the state with the exception of unity schools which should be funded by the Federal Government.
    c. Tertiary education should be appropriately priced and fees charged to partially recover cost.
    d. Government should provide grants, loans and scholarships for the needy and gifted students; provide basic infrastructure and support research.
11. Fund and support research on oral tradition and contemporary history.
12. Promote indigenous book production in all fields and promote a reading culture and the use of libraries; encourage the writing of books for the citizenry, especially the young; underscoring the importance of these values.
13. Ensure that funding of primary and secondary levels of education takes priority over tertiary education. Primary and secondary levels should be free while tertiary levels should charge fees to partially recover costs.

14. Allocate not less than 26% of the national (federal, state and local governments) budget to education and deploy not more than 20% of the education budget to administrative expenditure and overheads.
15. Make computer education compulsory in all schools in the Federation.
16. Fight examination malpractice and other youth crimes by using the Parents-Teachers Associations, WAI Brigade and the electronic and print media.
17. Strictly enforce free and compulsory primary education and rid our schools of cultism.
18. Provide short training (in principles and practices of education) to NYSC members during camp and assign them to local schools as required.
19. Reform the primary and secondary education curricula, technical and vocational skills agenda, science, mathematics, computer science and technology content to ensure that school leavers meet the standards required for the nation's development. Provide continuous independent inspection and take effective remedial action where necessary.
20. Establish institution to absorb JSS 3 graduates who can not go on to SSS under apprenticeship schemes. Treat such institutions as secondary educational institutions and link them with vocational schools, mass literacy and adult education and other programmes.
21. Organise excursions and exchange programmes amongst schools; introduce entrepreneurship development programmes in schools, starting from the secondary to the tertiary educational level.
22. Restructure and make tertiary educational institutions efficient:
    a. Emulate successful private sector programmes such as sourcing non-core services and streamlining internal processes.
    b. Rationalise the number of supervisory institutions, educational institutions and programmes.
    c. Introduce activity-based costing and effective internal auditing.
    d. Determine the level of service to be provided by tertiary educational institutions, to ensure that they meet international standards and the associated level of public funding that can

be afforded on a sustainable basis to maintain the quality of service.
   e.   Solicit private and public sector groups for students.

23. Establish facilities in universities and polytechnics for training in technology acquisition and small and medium scale enterprises management schemes.

Conclusion
Let the realisation dawn on all of us that the future leaders of Nigeria, as it has been said often, are the Nigerian children. This should not be a "lip-talk" but one of commitment to its actual realisation.

There is no special child, for all the children are special because each is endowed with a talent with which to contribute meaningfully to the development of Nigeria.

The transformation of a society for the better begins with a profound educational foundation for the children. This ingredient for national transformation was captured by Professor Wole Soyinka in his speech delivered recently at the annual meeting of the World Bank and the International Monetary Fund in Washington D. C., U.S.A.

In it, he said creative liberation is the best index for measuring economic growth and development and not gross national product. And this creative liberation can only come about through exploring and nurturing of human skills.

The following are some quotations from his speech in which he painted the picture of a society — Palermo of Sicily, Italy — which rose from a complete human and cultural ruins caused by a tyrannised reign, to a conspicuous transformation, restoring its cultural and human values with the children being educated to play a prominent role in manifesting this.

This serves as a good example to Nigeria which has gone through a period of similar tyrannised, oppressed reign, during which the human, cultural, educational and economic values were bastardised and destroyed:

> ...that what we should understand as development must move away from emphasis on Gross National Product and revert to the human scale to be measured in the exploration and nurturing of skills within a social condition that fully liberate such skills ... would discover a

> vast release of the reservoir of productive potential as a result of the atmosphere of increased freedom and the elimination of arbitrary bondage.
>
> And it helps us to differentiate between culture as understood, or as projected, on the one hand — as a kind of glamorised occasion that merely seek to deodorise a reality of civic alienation, lend spurious prestige to the violent overleads of a captive domain, and, on the other, the culture of participation, of social mobilisation that was initiated.
>
> ...the complete transformation of the mentality of defeatism in the old generation, side by side with the nurturing of a new generation in the principle of the very human ordinariness and entitle of creativity and democracy.
>
> ...the programme of creative liberation is the profoundest of any form of investment in humanity and humanity is the sole end and purpose of the project of material development project within any society.

What other better way than this is there to emphasise on the importance of education in nurturing and liberating human skills for material development of a country? Suffice it to say, education is the first task, the only means to expose the potential skill of any human being.

It is imperative for all to bear this in mind: an African, a Nigerian in particular, is practical in nature right from the origin. This has long been his basis for survival and development. Relatively, science and technology which require a bit of theory and more of practical shouldn't be alien to an African or a Nigerian as it is in his nature to practise and discover or invent. Our systems seemed to collapse because we derailed from our basic nature to survive and grow, and relied upon intellectual theory which has led to physical laziness. We have not been able to combine the two, mental and physical qualities to produce results. Until we revert to this basic nature and integrate this culture into our system of education, we will continue to fail in attaining our goals in educational, economic, and social development.

REFERENCES

Coleman, J.S. 1968. "The concept of equality of educational opportunity." *Harvard Educational Review,* 38 (1):7-22.

Cornish, E. 1980. *The Study of the Future.* Washington, DC: World Future Society.

Fantini, M.D. 1976. *Alternative Education.* New York: Doubleday & Company Inc.

Federal Republic of Nigeria. 1975. *The Third National Development Plan (1975-1980).* Lagos: Federal Ministry of Economic Development.

Goslin, D.A. 1965. *The School in Contemporary Society.* Glenview, Illinois: Scott, Foregman & Co.

Hostrop, R.W. 1975. *Education Beyond Tomorrow.* Homewood, Illinois: ETC Publications.

Kauffman, D.L. 1976. *Teaching the Future: A Guide to Future-Oriented Education.* Palm Springs, Ca: ETC Publications.

LaConte, R.T. and LaConte, E. 1975. *Teaching Tomorrow Today: A Guide to Futuristics.* New York: Bantam.

Morrish, I. 1976. *Aspects of Educational Change.* London: George Allen and Unwin.

Shane, H.G. 1973. *The Educational Significance of the Future.* Bloomington, Indiana: Phi Delta Kappa Educational Foundation.

Taiwo, C.O. 1980. *The Nigerian Educational System: Past, Present and Future.* Lagos: Thomas Nelson (Nig.) Ltd.

Toffler, A. 1970. *Future Shock.* New York: Random House.

Toffler, A. 1972. *The Futurists.* New York: Random House.

Toffler, A. 1974. *Learning for Tomorrow: The Role of the Future in Education.* New York: Random House.

Ukeje, B.O. 1975. "Pedagogical Problems in Nigeria Today." *Presence Africaine,* 95: 301-320.

Index

Abject poverty, 124-125
Abnormalities, 61-62
Abstract thought, 67
Academic
— programmes, 137
— skills, 145
Acceptance and Obedience, 51
Accomplishment v. Inferiority (6 to 11 years), 44, 106
Acquisition of knowledge and skills (mechanism) theory, 41
Action Plan on Education, 222-225
Adaptation, 47
Administrative Policy, 150
Adolescence (12 to 16 years), 60-61, 67
Adult authority, 51
Affective-interactionist, 147
African
— Charter on the Right and Welfare of the Child, 204
— Network for the Prevention and Protection Against Child Abuse and Neglect (ANPPCAN), 126, 200, 202
Age designations, 47
Aid, 203
— major schemes of, 203
Aide, 93
Alcoholism, 121

Allocating Funds, 193-194
Amnesty International Report, 124
Amortisation Loan Scheme, 218, 220-222
Ancient education, 10
Appearance (of Teachers), 91
Apprenticeship schemes, 224
Arabic — Language, 184
— Schools, 184
Armed Forces Ruling Council (AFRC), 186
Art
— equipment and materials required, 176-177
Articles pertaining to education, 17
Attained tests, 19
Attitude, 91
Audio-visual — aids, 211
— Equipment, 166
Auditory and Hearing Disabilities, 75
Autonomy v. Shame and doubt (2 to 3 years), 43, 106

Baby sales business, 124
Back talk, 24
Basic Communication Skills, 212
Behaviour of the child, 23-25
Behavioural decay, 139
Behaviourism, 42
Behaviourist-theoretical, 148
Beijing rules, 199

Better Life Programme, 198, 207
Blocks and Building Structures, 170-171
Budget, 190-191
Budgetary allocation, 204
Budgeting, 189-191
— allocation, 203
Business Policy, 150

Career
— education, 212
— guidance, 212
— opportunities, 92
Casual Learning, 34
Certificate of immunization, 13
Characteristics of Result-oriented Policies, 149-150
Child Abuse
— causes of, 123-125
— kinds of, 122-123
— meaning of, 120-121
Child Abuse and Neglect, 121-123, 125-126
Child
— development, 93
— stages of, 57-77, 95
— Education
— aim of, 8
— tasks for, 7-8
— instruction, 191
— Labour, 16, 120, 125, 127-133, 210
— causes of, 129-130
— definition of, 127
— on the child
— effects of, 130-133
— Personal Policy, 150
— rearing, 123
— Study, 18-21
— methods of, 19
— tests of, 19-20

— Welfare Services, 207
Childhood (2 to 12 years), 60, 67
Children
— and Young Persons Law, 1958, 199
— juvenile delinquency, 143
Children's
— experiences in school, 33
— market, 124-125
Child's total environment, 42
Christian missionaries, 184
Chronological age, 72
Cinematography Act, 1990, 199
Class promotion, 41
Classification and Relationship Skills, 49-50
Classified children, 206
Classroom
— activities, 113
— favouritism, 25
— Life, 107
— manager, 92
— observation, 52
— programme, 92
Closed system of learning, 41-42
Closed theory, 40
Codes of behaviour, 6
Cognitive
— development, 49, 133
— interactionist, 147
— self, 84
Colleges of Education, 13
Committing to memory, 39
Community Resources (Excursion), 180
— list of places, 180-181
Company manners, 27
Competition, 52
Computer
— Age, 154
— Assisted Instruction (CAJ), 167
— forms of, 167-168
— education, 224
— literacy, 166

— Programming, 167
Concrete operational stage 9 7 to 11 years), 47-49
Conditioning, 36-37
Conflict with Parents, 138
Continuous Assessment, 153-156
Convention on the Elimination of All forms of Discrimination Against Women, 142
Conventions on the Rights of the child, 17-18, 199
— programmes for implementation, 200-201
— ratification of, 198-199
Creating Public Awareness, 201-202
Creative
— dance, 105
— liberation
— physical education, 104-105
— self, 84
Creativity, 107
Crediting of Income, 194
Criminal Law, 199
Cross-cultural education, 107
Cult, 136-137
— definition of, 136
— practices, 136
Cultism, 210
Cultural
— environment, 107
— policy on education, 205
— activities on, 205
Curriculum, 83-91
— Analysis chart, 84
— guidelines, 203
— materials, 50
— programme, 85

Daily Plan Chart, 84
Dancing, 105
Day
—/Boarding Schools, 159-162
— Care, 31

— centres, 202-203
— programmes, 31
— of African child, 201
— school system, 160-161
Declaration of the Rights of the child, 142
Deliberate learning, 34
Democratisation of education, 12
Demonstration, 39
Descriptive research data, 52
Development
— general principles and theories of, 42-43
— Theories
— basic philosophies from, 147-148
Developmental — maturationist, 148
— theorists, 43
Diagnostic tests, 19
Direct and free Ordering, 195
Discrimination, 206-207
Donor agencies, 203
Drill and Practice, 167
Dropout children, 133
Dropouts, 132, 137, 155
Drug
— definition of, 133
Drug Abuse, 16, 133-136
— causes of, 134
— solution, 135-136
Drug
— addiction, 120-121, 133, 135, 210
— trafficking, 133
— and addiction, 141
Drugs
— types of, 135

Early
— child education, 163-164
— child Education Programmes
— nature of planning and administering, 151-152

— Childhood Education, 29-32, 77, 80, 85, 93, 135, 203
— childhood
   — learning, 85
   — programme, 30-31, 105
— education programmes, 30, 145, 166
   — goals and objectives of, 145-147
— girl child marriage, 141
— marriage, 129, 141

Education
— and Advancement of Girls/Women, 142-143
— counsellor, 93
— funds, 185, 188
   — disbursement of, 188-189
— philosophy
   — definition of, 145
— Policy
   — and Programmes, 200-202
   — inconsistency in, 158-159
— rates, 186
— Tax Decree, 188-187
— Tax Fund, 192, 218
   — Approach, 220-221
   — how it works, 221-222

Educational
— aims, 2
— charges and fees
   — introduction of, 213
— deprivation, 132
— funds, 216
— goals, 92
— objective, 163
— Problems, 152-162
— programmes, 163, 191, 216
— status, Access and Utilisation, 131-133

— System, 155
— technology, 211
— television, 211
— Vouchers, 193

Egocentric speech, 49
Elite children, 206-207
Emotional
— Abuse, 122, 128
— development, 105
   — stages of, 105-107
— health, 107
— neglect, 122-123
— self, 84
— Traits, 107

Environment
— and Mental Development, 69
— and Physical Development, 62

Environmental stimulation, 30
Equipment and materials, 163-182
Erikson's Theory
— educational implications of, 46

Establishing Policies, 148
Evaluation of learning, 41
Exam - test system, 155
Examination malpractices, 140, 143
Exceptional Child (Handicapped and Gifted), 74
Exploitation of children, 127-128

Family
— environment, 122
— Planning, 126
— responsibilities, 138
— Support Programme, 201, 207
— tradition, 129
— Value system
   — sensitivity to, 110

Federal Government Colleges, 206
Female genital mutilation (FGM), 141-142
Financial
— Appropriation and

Accountability, 216
— Control and Monitor, 213-214
— Misappropriation, 209-210
— Problems, 156-158
Financing education, 184-196
Fist-fights, 25
Five-Year-Old children, 54
Formal
— education, 1, 130, 137
— operational stage (7 to 14 years), 47, 50
— thought, 49
Foster parents, 122
Foul language, 24
Four-Year-Old Children, 53-54
Free
— Basic Education, 203-204
— education scheme, 162
Functional Classification of Budget, 191
Furniture (for schools), 164-165
Future
— School curriculum, 212
— Schools
— financing of, 212

Games, 167
Gender Violence, 140-143
Generativity v. Stagnation (Middle Age), 45
Genetic factors, 43
Genius, 68
Gifted children, 74, 77-78, 220
Gifted/exceptional children, 154
Girl - child education, 204
Girls trafficking for prostitution, 141
Good-for-nothing children, 137, 155
Grants-in-aid, 184
Grassroots, 214-215
— enlightenment, 215
Guided discovery, 38
Guilt and punishment, 51

Handicapped
— and gifted schools, 13
— children, 77, 178
Health and Safety in Nursery School
— promotion of, 99
Health Problem, 130-131
Heredity — and environment, 20-21, 62, 72
— and Mental Development, 68
— and Physical Development, 61-62
HIV/AIDS, 141
Home
— condition, 130, 134
— learning, 211
— visit, 109-110
House-keeping and Dramatic Play, 171-172
Human rights violation, 139
Humanistic Psychology, 42

Identity v. Confusion (12 to 18 years), 44-45
Imaginary child, 20
Immunisation records, 99
Implementation of policy and programmes, 214-215
Imprest Accounts, 195
In-service programmes, 91
Incest, 123
Individual conference, 111
Individualised learning systems, 211
Industrial Revolution Age, 211
Infancy (birth to 2 years), 60, 67
Infectious diseases, 131
Information
— revolution, 212-213
— Revolution Age, 211
Initiation rites, 1
Initiative v. Guilt (4 to 5 years), 44, 156
Innate Tendencies of Man, 21-23, 33
Insight Learning, 38-39

Insurance policy, 13
Instructional materials, 13, 155
   — inadequacy of, 155
Integrity v. Despair (Old Age), 45-46
Intellectual
   — activity, 68
   — development, 47
        — major stages of, 47
Intelligence, 71-74
   — quotient (I.Q.), 72-73, 75, 77
   — tests, 19
Intelligent learning, 38
Interactionism, 41-42
International
   — agencies, 209
   — convention agreements, 142
   — Year of the Family (IYF), 201
Intimacy v. Isolation (Young Adulthood), 45
Item classification of Budget, 191

Junior Secondary Education, 202

Kindergarten
   — and nursery schools, 164-165
   — education, 30-31

Language, 49
   — Arts, 168
        — equipment and materials required, 168-169
   — Skills, 34, 67
Learning
   — and development, 32-33
   — and teaching methods, 212
   — as whole, 39
   — attitudes and habits, 37
   — by association or conditioning, 37
   — by Imitation, 39
   — definition of, 34
   — Disabilities, 74-75
   — environment, 33, 41, 113, 161, 196
   — evaluation of, 41
   — experiences, 42, 50, 85
   — materials, 38
   — process 33, 36-41, 160, 166, 219
   — skills, 212
   — system, 41
   — Theories, 32, 40-42
Legislation
   — skills, 26
   — vocabulary, 55
Local
   — Education Authority (LEA), 187, 189-190, 193-195, 214-216
   — Government Areas (LGAs), 215
   — Property Tax, 191-192

Malnutrition, 131, 133
Management and financing education
   — policy for 186-187
Manners, 26-27
Mass Mobilisation for Social Justice, Self Reliance and Economic Recovery (MAMSER), 200
Mass retrenchment and unemployment, 122, 126
Maternal and child care, 198
Mathematics
   — equipment and materials required, 169-170
Maturation, 62-63
Media Role, 202
Memorisation, 36, 39
   —principles of, 39-40

Mental
— ability, 41, 68
— age, 72-73
— development, 46-47, 63-69, 71, 136-137
    — degeneration of, 132
    — factors of, 47
    — Stages in, 63-68
— exercise, 73
— handicap, 74
— Health, 105-107
    — fostering of, 105-107
    — problems, 105
— Maturation, 69-71
— Retardation, 75
Micro-computer Equipment
    — guidelines for, 168
Micro-computers, 166-168
Misfit children, 133
Misfits, 137
Mission schools, 184-185
Moral standards, 6
Mortality rate of children
    — decline of, 129
Mother tongue, 205
Motivation, 35, 41
Motor activity, 63-64
Motor control, 67
Movement Education, 104
Music
    — equipment and materials required, 175-176

National
    — Child Rights Implementation Committee, 200
    — Child Welfare Committee, 199
    — Children's and Youth Day celebration, 201
    — Children's holiday camp, 201
    — Commission for Nomadic Education, 204
    — Commission for Women, 1989, 200
    — Commission of Primary Education, 187
    — Committee on Women and children, 200
    — Council on Education, 156
    — Policy on Education, 12, 152-153, 155, 198, 202
    — Policy on Health, 198
    — Policy on Population, 198
    — Primary Education Commission, 203
    — Primary Education Fund, 186
    — Working Committee on Child Welfare, 200

Natural laws, 3
Never-do-wells, 137
New
    — National Policy on Education, 14
    — Skills, 212
Nigeria Labour Act, 199
Nigerian — Children's Trust Fund, 201
    — Mass Media, 126
Nomadic
    — children, 210
    — Education, 204, 210
Non-availability of Facilities and Equipment, 155-156
    — Discrimination on Educational Activities, 215-216
    — Governmental Organisation (NGO), 135, 202, 209, 223
    — grassroots Implementation, 207, 209
    — Implementation, 153-155

— verbal behaviour, 26
Normative - descriptive data, 52
Numbers, 51
Nursery School, 32
NYSC members, 224

OAU Charter on the Right and Welfare of the Child, 199-200
Occupational
— choices, 46
— Hazards, 131
— Stress, 134
— training, 75
Open
— education movement, 50
— System, 42
— theory, 40
Oral language, 27
Organisation, 47
Orthopaedic Problems, 76-77

Parent
— child relationship, 120
— child role, 122
— Teacher Association (PTA), 214, 224
— Conference, 113
— levies, 184
Parental
— disciplinary practices, 129
— influence, 24
Parents
— Policy, 151
— Teachers-Students Seminars, 215
Participatory experience, 85
Pattern Learning, 40
Peer Group
— Influence, 134
— Pressure, 138
Perceptual
— motor activities, 100-104

— motor equipment and materials, 179
Personality
— development, 43-46
— tests, 20
Physical
— Abuse, 122
— and oral responsiveness, 107-108
— development, 57-63, 65, 100, 105, 132
— stages in, 57-61
— education, 104-105
— activities, 75
— health examination, 13
— Maturation, 62-63, 67
— self, 84, 99-104
— development of, 99-104
— skills, 212
Physically handicapped, 74
Physiological revolution, 44
Piaget's
— Stages, 47
— States of Cognitive Development, 46-50
— Theory
— educational implication of, 50-55
— of Cognitive development, 50
Planned Parenthood Federation of Nigeria, 126
Platform for Action of the Fourth World Conference on Women, 142
Play, 85
Policies
— categories of, 150-151
Political Violence, 124
Poverty, 129-130, 139
Practical Lesson in Schools
— benefits of, 218-220
Praise words, 27
Praises, 27

Pre
— marriage counselling, 126
— natal environment, 62
— natal (from conception to birth), 59, 66
— operational stage (2 to 7 years), 47-51
— primary education, 12
— school programme, 83
Prerequisites for Efficient Learning, 34-36
Principles of Learning, 33-34
Professional Library, 181
Programmed Learning, 211
Property Tax Fund, 192
Prostitution, 120, 137-140, 210
Psychological State, 120
Psychosocial
— Development, 43-46
— Hazards, 131
Public Relations Policy, 151
Punishments and rewards, 37
Purchasing Guidelines, 163-164

Rational thinking, 42
Rationalism, 42
Raw or Primitive materials, 179
Readiness, 34-35, 62
Reading, 70
Record Policy, 151
Recreation Facilities for Schools, 182
Relaxation and tension relieving activities, 104
Religious instruction, 7
Remembering by heart, 39
Repeated experiences, 36
Research studies, 204
Reversibility, 48
Right of the child, 16-27
Rights of the Child Programmes, 207
Ritual (of Teachers), 92-93
Rude society, 160
Rules and Games, 51
Rural schools, 207

Science
— and Technology Policy, 202
— education, 203
— equipment and materials required, 172-173
Scholastic Achievement, 130
School
— activities, 108
— Bank Accounts, 195-196
— behaviour of children, 24
— community, 106, 218-219
— culture, 159
— curriculum, 114
— environment, 91, 110
— fees, 184-185
— Finances
— suggestions on, 216-217
— Financial Operations, 194-196
— Funds
— sources of, 217-218
— programmes, 108
Schools of the future, 211-212
Self
— assertion and control, 106
— expression, 105
— help activities, 134
— help skills, 75
— identity, 136
— solving problems activities, 41
Sense of Identity, 107
Sensory Integration and Experience, 100
Sexual
— abuse, 122-123
— exploitation of children, 16, 142
— maturity, 60
Sign Language, 75
Simulation, 167
Sinking Fund Scheme, 218, 220-222
6-3-3-4 educational structures/system, 153-154, 203

Six-Year-Old Children, 55
Slave-like prostitution, 141
Social
— adventure, 138
— Behaviour, 51
— Development Policy for Nigeria, 198
— education, 212
— environment, 21
— hostility, 132
— ills, 120
— interaction, 50
— problem, 136
— self, 84
— studies, 170
— vices, 160, 219
— violence, 120-143
— welfare office, 126
Socialisation, 30, 127, 129
Special
— education, 77
— schools, 13, 154, 222
— establishment of, 204
Speech and Language Disorders, 76
Spiritual bankruptcy, 121
Staff Primary Schools Management Board, 187
Street Hawking, 128-129, 161
Students' Working environment, 44

Table manners, 27
Teacher
— child relationship, 33
— Parent Conferences, 110-118
— Parent Relationship, 107-110
Teachers, 91
— personal qualities for therapeutic climate, 95-96
— Registration Council, 223
— Roles, 93-95
Teaching

— aid materials, 156
— aids, 188
— methods, 98-104
— techniques, 95
Technical schools, 13
Technological transformation, 211
Teen marriage, 141
Test System, 154
Theory
— meaning of, 40
Thinking and Reasoning, 51
Three-Year-Old Children, 52-53
Tobacco and alcohol advertisement decrees, 199
Toilet training, 106
Tradition and culture, 129
Traditional forms of education, 1
Training, 37, 70, 91
Transitional theory, 40, 42
Trial and Error Learning, 37-38
Truant of the worst order, 155
Trust v. Mistrust (birth to 1 year), 43, 105-106
Tutorial Approach, 167

UN Convention on the Rights of the Child, 200
Unity Schools, 160-161, 206
Universal — Basic Education (UBE), 158
— Basic Education Policy, 158
— Declaration of Human Rights, 142
— Primary Education, 184
— (UPE) Scheme, 157-158, 185

Verbal
— Abuse, 122-123
— discussions and pictures, 85

— language-communicative
    speeches, 49
— mental images, 50
Vesico — Virginal Fistula (VVF), 141
Visible indication, 152
Vision 2010 on Education, 222-225
Visual Impairments, 76
Vocational
    — schools, 13
    — training, 132
WAI Brigade, 224
War on Poverty, 30
Water, Sand and Mud, 173-174
Whole Conference (PTA), 113-114
Wood-work or Carpentry, 174-175
Work accomplishment, 44

Working
    — age, 130
    — children, 132
World
    — Congress Against Commercial Sexual Exploitation of children, 142
    — Health Organisation (WHO), 105
    — Summit for children, 199, 201
Writing and Graphic, 167

Youth (16 to 21 years), 68

www.ingramcontent.com/pod-product-compliance
Lightning Source LLC
Chambersburg PA
CBHW070601300426
44113CB00010B/1348